50 Things Your Life Doesn't Need

50 Things Your Life Doesn't Need

Sam Davidson

TRADE PAPER
PRESS

Turner Publishing Company

445 Park Avenue, 9th Floor
New York, NY 10022
Phone: (212)710-4338   Fax: (212)710-4339

200 4th Avenue North, Suite 950
Nashville, TN 37219
Phone: (615)255-2665   Fax: (615)255-5081

www.turnerpublishing.com

50 Things Your Life Doesn't Need

Library of Congress Cataloging-in-Publication Data

Davidson, Sam, 1980-
   50 things your life doesn't need / Sam Davidson.
      p. cm.
   ISBN 978-1-59652-756-0
1. Conduct of life. 2. Self-realization. I. Title. II. Title: Fifty things your life doesn't need.

BF637.C5D37 2010
158.1--dc22

Printed in China

10 11 12 13 14 15 16 17—0 9 8 7 6 5 4 3 2 1

Nothing much happens without a dream. For something really great to happen, it takes a great dream.

~Robert Greenleaf

Contents

Acknowledgments

No book is ever written alone. Even though the author's name graces the cover and the accolades for the book are his, he could not have written it without the generous help of others. This book is proof that no writer goes about his craft in a vacuum.

Thanks to my parents, I have been able to pursue my passion of telling stories that need telling in order to motivate others to change the things that need changing. Their love and support of my craft began before I said my first sentence ("Tie shoes.") and will undoubtedly continue until I stop talking.

Thanks to my wife and daughter, I have felt more love and support than one man deserves. That feeling has been a rock in my personal storms of uncertainty while writing this book. I do nothing in my life without the two of them in mind, whether it's changing jobs, writing a book, or indulging a new passion. Being a husband and father are my foremost identities and to be great at both of them is my life's highest ambition.

Thanks to Ben Grier, this book has a title, became properly organized, and was written with a clear purpose in mind. He read it more than he should have, not because he felt obligated, but because he is an enduring friend.

Thanks to Angie Gore, my ideas became a book. Her support throughout the project has allowed me to focus on developing the core ideas, which I hope will inspire people to begin to live life with passion, unencumbered by everything they don't need.

Thanks to the team at Turner Publishing, this resource will be a reality. From editing to marketing to production, the team is a professional organization that aims to publish books that enable people to live better lives.

Thanks to countless others for their love and support throughout this process, I was able to get where I am today. From founding a company intent on saving the world, to producing apparel and merchandise that makes a difference for communities across the U.S., I have been honored to be a teammate with some of the most passionate people on the planet. You are my inspiration, and proof that anyone can find their passion and live a life full of it.

———————

To Lynnette and Lindley. If it all comes down to one thing, you two are it.

Introduction

This isn't a book about stuff. It's a book about passion. It's a book about priorities. It's a book about you and the kind of life you want to live and the kind of person you want to be.

Very few of us have dared to think about the kinds of lives we really want to live. We claim we can't find time for quiet reflection or deep introspection. Daily responsibilities and routines demand our attention, leaving no time for self-discovery. Modern technology, countless forms of entertainment, and many other distractions also combine to keep us from figuring out what the point of all of it is.

As a result, we fill our houses with things, buying whatever it is that's new on the shelves or carries a promise of self-improvement or a glimmer of hope that we can be a better, happier person. Before too long, however, our homes are filled with things and our hearts are empty of meaning. In a brief moment of inspiration, we find empty boxes to fill with the things we no longer want or use, thinking the extra space will give us room to breathe and that in this way maybe tomorrow will be different.

But it isn't. The inspiration is temporary and before long, new things replace the old things and we clean out again and then press repeat. The solution isn't less stuff. The answer is more passion.

As for books about passion themselves, there are far too many already, promising easy plans for finding ways to land dream jobs, live a life of leisure, and be famous, all for one low price. Those books may work for lots of people, but I've found that they don't work for someone like me. Their ambitious words seem to fall short in a real world full of real commitments.

Whether you're a full-time dad trying to teach your children to be honest, loving, and caring people, or whether you're trying your hardest to climb the ladder as fast and as far as you can, I think this book can offer you something those other books may not. That's because if each of us were willing to pause for just a moment and ask ourselves what we'd really like to do with our one life, the answer would probably be the same. We want to do something, but not just anything. We want to do something *remarkable*. We want to do something meaningful, something lasting and with impact. We want to do something that fulfills us and something that makes us excited to wake up each day. We also want to be someone important. We want to be someone who's loved and is loving. We want to be great friends and caring parents. We want to be recognized, appreciated, and memorable, even after we're gone.

Each of us has only one life. What will you do with yours?

Everyone wants to live a life in which a passion can be pursued, whether it's through a career or after work. But many people, including you, may claim you don't exactly know what that passion is. It's very difficult to follow something if you're not sure what it looks like.

This book will help you find your passion. Many people claim that they'd love to find what they're passionate about and then live out that passion every day, if only they had the time and convenience to discover it. You may have found yourself claiming the same thing. Maybe you even went so far as to go "off the grid" for a few weeks, trying to get away from it all so that you could figure out what it's all about.

Perhaps that quick vacation helped. It probably didn't. You went back to work, repeated your daily routine, and did things exactly as you'd always done them. You may have discovered an interest or a fleeting hobby while you were trying to find your passion, but when you returned to your regular life, all of its distractions stopped you from pursuing the interest or hobby that you discovered in that fortnight.

The problem is that we have too many things—too much stuff—distracting us, daring us to let it go and pursue our hidden passion. We all have certain responsibilities based on our place in life. You may be a parent or a spouse, a boss or a neighbor—titles that are significant to you and challenge you to be a better person. If you derive meaning from these titles, then they don't need to be eschewed just so that you can have fun finding a passion.

Chances are, these titles don't even stand in the way of finding and living your passion. They carry some sort of importance with them that in turn motivates you in a particular way. What stands in the way of finding and living your passion are things: Distractions. Diversions. Disposable stuff. Those are what your life doesn't need.

What follows in these pages are 50 things you'll need to get rid of in order to find the time, energy, money, and other resources to discover your passion and then live a life that is in line with it. By following these suggestions and the other tools for finding your passion, you will be freed to live passionate-ly—perhaps for the very first time.

A nice round number, 50 is a manageable amount. We can count to fifty in less than a minute, there are fifty states in the U.S., and many of us can still fill our gas tanks on a fifty-dollar bill (with nostalgia for the days of fifteen. Alas). The number 50 is thus a good metaphor for just how far we can get from truly living. The world moves so fast today that it's easy to accumulate distractions that aren't essential to living a passionate life. Getting rid of these things is no small feat. It may take you a year, or you may be able to wrap it up in a few months, but completing the list is a worthy commitment. Will you be able to get rid of all 50 things in this book?

Things: Ever since the beginning of the Indus-trial Revolution, our world has been mass-producing stuff on an ever-growing scale, and the more of it that can be produced the poorer in quality it often seems to become. Factories churn out toys and gad-gets made of metal and plastic, and marketers find just the right language and opportunity to sell it all to us for a price we can't refuse. But in the end, all we're buying are things. A thing defined as "stuff" is something that doesn't have significance. Stuff is a space filler. The word itself is so vague as to be meaningless, slapped into a sentence to describe any*thing* from a coffee cup to a poster to a car. As a result, our lives are full of things and empty of meaning. Meaning should be paramount. Things in the form of stuff can be tossed aside and we'll barely notice a difference.

Your life: This book is about you. Many of the things on the list are things I have eliminated to free up time and resources to live a passionate life. That passionate life has been a rewarding one to live, taking me to places I never imagined, to meet people I admire deeply. Your life, however, is not my life; the passion you discover as a result of reading this book will be uniquely yours. I offer examples of what you may discover when you get rid of all of these things, but it will be up to you to discover how the exercise benefits you personally. Whether your passion is to invent a better cell phone battery or teach dance lessons to senior citizens, it will be yours and yours alone to be lived out as you see fit. I have written this book to apply to all circumstances, whether you have just graduated from college or are looking for a mid-career transition. Each thing—as well as the six questions to help you find your passion (see the Conclusion to the book)—can be applied by anyone in any station of life. It's up to you to live the life you want, one that I hope is dedicated to your passion.

Doesn't need: We all understand what the word *need* means. There are only a few needs for survival that humans have—food, water, shelter. I may add things like community and purpose to the list, but those categories are not basic to survival. None of the 50 things on the list are things you must have to survive. They may be things you want, but if you're honest when you read them and dedicated when you rid your life of them, you'll realize that you don't die without them. You won't starve, suffer, or lose your sanity after working through this list. Best of all, you'll gain time, money, motivation, and resources to then go discover your true passion in life. And that's what you really need—a clearly articulated passion around which to base your life.

Is it all really about passion?

Don't start reading this book hoping that you'll find ways to clean out your closet. Start by taking stock of what's important, what you value. Once you have correctly identified what matters, you will find it easier to define what it is your life doesn't need. If you simply start with a bag meant for the salvage store, and don't figure out what it is that really matters to you, then you'll need to reread this book every few months and refill the bag. Rather than focusing on what you don't mind discarding, I want you to discover what stirs you, excites you, motivates you, and ignites you. I want you to find your passion.

You'll see the word *passion* a lot in these pages. It's an overused word, but I'm a fan of overused words. I created a company and lifestyle brand based on the word *cool,* after all. What we developed in just four years at Cool People Care, however, was a community of people who believe that it's cool to care. In a world where countless messages convince people that you can be cool based upon what kind of car you drive, soft drink you enjoy, or shirt you wear, we set out to convince the world that *caring* is the cool thing to do.

I see passion in a similar light. No one thinks that living a passionate life is a bad thing or an unworthy pursuit. But, too often living a passionate life is equated with making lots of money or being able to spend two weeks every month on the beach. If your passion takes you to either of those end points and you're ecstatic and fulfilled by it, go for it. But it's important to know from the start that finding your passion isn't about making money or living a life of leisure. It's about living a life of meaning.

I think it's important to use the word *passion* hundreds of times in these pages because of its familiarity, but with the hope that I can help you redefine it and begin to see this word and all it can mean in a whole new way. Even though the word may be overused and oversold, there are not enough passionate individuals in the world today. Or maybe there are not enough people who are passionate about the right things. By simply going to a professional football game, you'll see 75,000 passionate people. The same goes for walking into a church service or a movie theater. We all have passions, but often they're not connected to something deeper within us—something that guides us to be our best selves and use that passion in the service of others and our community.

The world is too big, too mysterious, too phenomenal, and too wonderful to be experienced without passion. Finding your passion and beginning to use it in service to the world (beginning with your own life and community) will unlock a new excitement within you—something dormant for far too long.

Before you dive into the list of 50 things that your life doesn't need, I need to share a few provisos about passion, warnings and advice to remember before you begin to find more time and opportunities to pursue yours. Remember these four guidelines as you begin to simplify your life so that you will head down the right path when it's time to begin to articulate your passion.

1. Your passions will change. First of all, think of your passions like best friends—you'll have a few throughout your lifetime and the best ones will stick with you, transcending age and geography.

My best friends up until the time I was thirteen years old included people like Jeremy, Drew, and Alan. I have no idea where those guys are now. But I do know where college friends Brad, Matt, Ben, and Adam are. Sure, part of that is getting older, the proliferation of digital communication, and deeper shared life experiences. But, it's also finding a kinship with someone that grows into a deep bond.

Your passions will be the same. Some may exist only for a season, right when you need them most. Others will grip you and be a part of your life forever. It will be okay to let go of ones that are no longer compatible. And it will be okay to stake a claim on those that touch you deep within.

It's important to understand, then, that above all else, you are loyal to yourself, not to a single passion. When you discover and define your passion after having read this book, be sure to write it down, tell others, and begin to live it. Just don't grow too fond of it. Be willing to let it go when you feel much more deeply about something else that meets the same criteria for being a passion. Embrace new life experiences and circumstances that have the potential to redefine your passion. Events like getting married, getting divorced, having children, and moving to a new city could all radically alter your passions. This is okay.

Because of this, you will discover and rediscover your passions. Some will ebb and flow with the circumstances of everyday life. And because finding your passion is a process, it's something you'll repeat. You may want to schedule time each year to revisit what it is you're passionate about and see if it continues to grow within you. Or, you may find that the passion is no longer there and a new one has taken its place.

You may have a *Eureka!* moment when you discover your passion. As protective as you may be of your passion when that happens, know that you will have other such moments. Those moments will happen not only when you discover another passion within you, but also when you rediscover a passion you once had. Like the high school flame you may never forget, your passion could continue to enter your mind from time to time.

2. You can have too many passions. Passions can be like pancakes—three or four sound great, but after a dozen, you'll feel sick to your stomach.

We weren't meant to handle too many passions. Maybe this is why days have only twenty-four hours and we should be sleeping for eight of them. Or maybe this is why we must never shirk our responsibilities to our families, our friends, and our mortgage company. Trying to chase every passion will leave us ignoring other things we need to focus on.

This is also why some passions may be right for certain seasons of life. Even if you discover your deep, abiding passion tomorrow, you may need to wait a few years before you can really begin to pursue it.

Many college students I meet, when telling me what they're passionate about, begin to list as many things they like as possible. When I notice this, I ask them to start writing them down, and very quickly they see how absurd it is to claim to have a dozen or more passions. Many of what they consider passions are mere interests, things they'd enjoy reading about, but not ideas they'd like to shape a life around. If you begin to feel as though you have more than three or four passions, I recommend that you make a list of them. Examine that list and determine what it is you'd actually like to stake a job, reputation, or decade on. Which of them actually stir something deep within you? I bet you'll find that only a few on your list make the cut.

3. Your passion is not an end in itself. Your passion is a compass, not a map. It will not spell out for you every step to take on your journey. Rather, it will point you in a general direction, which means you will have to be flexible as to how you get there.

When we were first married, my wife would cringe when we traveled. I never mapped out directions beforehand. Rather, I assumed that road signs would take us where we were headed, and that without a map, we were more inclined to explore places we'd never been before. After trying to find our hotel on our first anniversary while it was dark and raining, I promised to myself that I would begin mapping out directions.

Although useful for vacationing, a map is not a good way to think about your passion. Your passion is meant to be vague. It's meant to be general. It's a bold vision that motivates you in every facet of life. As such, it can take different forms. It's your true north, holding you steady to where you'd like to go, but not offering specific turn-by-turn directions on how to get there.

Chances are, you will be charting new territory when it comes to your passion. Although another person may share your passion, that person's journey may have led down a road you're unwilling or unable to travel. Like early pioneers, you may have to venture into uncharted lands and make a way for yourself. It's okay to rely on the stories and examples of others as you begin to live your passion. But it's also okay—and even preferable—to blaze your own trail. Learn about how others found their passion, but don't try to retrace their journey step by step.

4. Your passion doesn't need to become your job. Society values those who have turned a passion into a profession. Building a company or starting a business centered on a singular passion seems to be the best and most valuable thing that one can do once a passion is found. This works for some, but it is not a good rule of thumb.

A word of warning: if you're only looking to find and live your passion because you hate your job and you want to earn a living doing what you (think you) love, you may end up no happier. Just because you love something doesn't mean you need to get paid to do it. Your passion may only be meant to be a leisurely pursuit. Perhaps your passion is only intended to be lived after work each day and on the weekends. Turning your passion into your profession might eventually even leave you resenting it.

Everyone wants a job they find fulfilling or challenging, but not everyone has to have such a job in order to be fulfilled. It's okay, in fact, to view your day job as a means to an end. Maybe it's how you pay the rent and all of your other bills in order to fully indulge your passion in life. Your passion may not even translate into a career. You may be passionate about basketball, but if you can't dunk, it will be difficult to find a way to earn money from the game. And while working for a team may seem like a match, you could find that concentrating on basketball all day every day robs it of its allure. In this case, it's better to keep your day job and save the money you need to watch your team play as often as you can.

If you are convinced that your passion should be your job, please also know that you will need much more than passion to turn this dream into reality. If you become an entrepreneur, you will enter a world of supply and demand, numbers and finances, rules and regulations. It may mean you work twice as many hours as you do now for half the pay. As romantic and enticing as a passion is, and despite all the claims that money follows those who follow their passion, it may issue no checks that you can use to pay your utility bill.

Therefore, as you begin to discover your passion, make sure you are realistic. Accept healthy doses of skepticism, whether it's from a concerned spouse or a doubting professor. Find a handful of people you know well and ask them to challenge you so that you don't end up losing everything else that means something to you. It's great to be passionate, but you'll also need a place to live.

Values this book is built on

This book was written with a set of ideas and values in mind. One would like to think such values are universal, but such an expectation would be naïve. As you look to find and live your passion, I believe the following concepts will be important to keep in mind. Even though passion is a solitary pursuit and this book is all about your life, these reminders will help shape your passion and its use in a well-rounded way:

Family. Each of us defines family differently, but we all have a network of people close to us whom we love, don't want to disappoint, and want to share as much of life with as possible. Make sure that your passionate life doesn't detract from these relationships. Build a business, simplify your life, pursue what means the most to you, but don't ignore or neglect those who love you the most. These will be the people who will help you achieve your wildest, most passionate dreams and the only people willing to pick you up if your dreams implode on you. Nothing can replace family, not even a very passionate life.

Community. Like family, your community is an important group of people who serve as a source of inspiration, comfort, and belonging. Unlike family, community will change throughout your life. As your passions take you to new and exciting places, you will form new and different communities.

Friends may come and go, but the notion of friendship should always be central in your life. It will allow you to keep your bearings and serve as a reminder that your passionate life is never lived alone.

Service. Once you discover your passion, its best expression may be in service to others. Giving of oneself to a cause or issue that needs attention is a very worthy endeavor. As you discover your passion, keep an open mind as to how you can use it to make the world a better place. You may find a fantastic nonprofit organization in your community that can use your passion to help its clients. Or you may find that your passion is perfectly suited to making an impact in the lives of young people. You don't have to focus 100 percent of your passion on the notion of community service, but devoting even a small percentage of it is a fantastic use of one's passion.

Time. Even though each of us was born into a different set of circumstances and may have different levels of material wealth, every single person on this planet has the same amount of time in a day. No matter how rich you may become or how advanced our society becomes, no one will be able to add minutes to an hour. It's a bank account we can't touch and we start to make withdrawals with our first breath on this planet. Therefore, it's important to understand how we can use our time wisely, both as we discover our passion and then, once we've discovered it, as we live it. Many of the items in the list of 50 things will free up time. You may use this extra time as you wish, but the passionate person will only use the extra time to indulge in more of the passion.

Resources. Each of us has different resources to our name, whether it's an amount of wealth or a particular talent. Although we'd like to believe we were all created equal, we know deep down this isn't the case. As such, rest assured that getting rid of the 50 things will free up resources in your life that you can use to find and live your passion. In some cases, discarding the things will help you save money, and in others, you'll find extra ideas, inspiration, tools, or examples. All of these added resources can be used to discover your passion.

And now, on to the list.

The 50 Things

– 1 –
No Self-examination:
Asking yourself the hard questions

Life is scary. It's scarier still when you have the willingness and fortitude to ask yourself the hard questions. Out of those difficult questions you will find your passions and what's important. But you have to be willing to confront yourself. Your life doesn't need to be lived unexamined.

Whether you stand in front of a mirror or pay to see a professional counselor, you need to find an activity and a time to examine who you are, what your values are, where you have failed, and what your biggest goals and ambitions are. You need to honestly ask yourself if you're happy, what needs modification in your life, and what's missing. You need to celebrate when you've been successful, be thankful about the incredible parts of your life, and hopeful about what the future may bring. In short, things may get emotional.

For some people, it's easy to put emotions and fears on hold and keep moving ahead. As long as you don't ask yourself if you're truly happy, you'll never be disappointed with the answer. But if you ask me, and as Plato said, the unexamined life is not worth living. If you are unhappy, uninspired, or unsuccessful, you can begin to take the steps toward rectifying the situation.

If you'd like to get started on this process, here are four questions to ask yourself at the end of every day. Doing so may lead to bigger revelations that are worth examining in even more detail, but these are a simple start:

1. When was I most successful today?
2. What disappointed me today?
3. What made me happiest today?
4. What was missing from today?

Ask yourself these questions (or some of your own) each day. Be honest with yourself when you do. The answers may startle you. Once you begin to look inside yourself, there is no telling what you will find. Eventually, however, you'll find your passion. When you're willing to look deep into your heart, you'll find a lot of things buried within, including the very things you're passionate about.

-- 2 --
Small dreams:
It's called dreaming for a reason

Abandon small dreams. Many small dreams, in fact, are not dreams at all. They are a to-do list, mere tasks you can accomplish by getting a second job or making an extra hour for them each day. Dream big dreams.

If you're in need of a dream—a really big one— here are five questions to ask yourself in order to dream a dream worth dreaming.

1. What do I like doing? Dreams are usually born out of a task you enjoy. The hopes you have for yourself, your family, and your community arise out of things you care about doing. What is it that you enjoy? What hobbies and pursuits make you happy?

2. What makes me angry? Dreams also take root when you see something that infuriates you. Maybe there is a law, a rule, or a policy you'd like to see overturned. Maybe you see an injustice that you would like to see stopped. The most famous of dreamers, Dr. Martin Luther King, Jr., had a dream take root out of something he saw that stirred him to action.

3. What could be? Dreams must be rife with possibility. You must be able to see a future, some sort of world that is different and better than the world of the here and now. What vision captures you? What do you hope takes root in the future— five, ten, or twenty years from now? You will need to articulate it.

4. Who needs help? Dreams come from seeing things you'd like to change based on something that angers or excites you, but they can also take shape and grow out of a desire to help others. Volunteers, parents, teachers, and change agents see a person or group of people that needs help and begin to dream up a solution or system to provide that help. Seeing a need will help you craft a dream to meet that need. What needs do you see near you?

5. *What am I good at?* Big dreams require time and energy, and rarely will you have a dream that demands you to spend that time and energy on something you have no talent for. Your skills and abilities will help control your dream and bring it to reality. What unique talent or gift do you possess? It could be the start of a great dream.

These questions are just the beginning and the first steps toward finding a big dream that's worth following. Keep asking these questions as you follow your dreams—one will become the core of your passion.

Untaken risks:
Parachutes are meant to be opened

Too many people sit on the sidelines, afraid to play the game of life because of fear of failure. As long as you don't try, you can't fail, so many think it's better to watch others get in the game, win, lose, and try all over again.

Nothing ventured, nothing gained. Risks were meant to be taken, and if you're not taking a handful of them every year, then you could be missing out on some fantastic rewards. I'm not suggesting taking out a second mortgage and putting it all on red in Vegas. And I'm not suggesting you drive without a seatbelt or while blindfolded. Rather, gauging appropriate risk and acting in light of it could build a renewed sense of purpose and allow you to accomplish things you've always dreamed of.

This may mean it's time to start a business, even if you could lose your entire investment. Maybe you should ask her to marry you, even if she says no. It might be time to pack up and move across the country, even if it takes six months to find a new job.

The only guarantee of a safer path is to take no risks. It's predictable, so the destination of a safe path is never anything other than what was promised from the start. So if you decide to stay on the straight and narrow, don't be surprised when you end up at the routine and boring. Even the safe path may turn out to be filled with risk. Gone are the days when Americans could count on working all their lives for the same company, followed by a comfortable retirement based on a pension and government Social Security.

It may sound ludicrous to quit your job, take a year off from college, or learn a new language. It may make no sense to spend your savings account, bring home a pet, or sell your car. But as long as you have a plan and the idea of an appropriate reward for having taken the risk, then it's time to leap.

Risk tolerance is different for each person. Depending upon your marital status, your values, and your stomach for laying it on the line, the types and frequency of the risks you take will vary. Some people can easily quit a full-time job to start a company; others may not be so willing. Others may jump at the chance to be on reality TV while the majority would rather watch and laugh.

The beauty of taking risks lies not only in the potential rewards that await, but also in the ease of restoration should things not work out. Time and again, people have built and rebuilt personal wealth and happiness to risk it all again when it made sense to dream another dream. Celebrating failure is okay—it allows you to learn from what went wrong so that you do not repeat the same mistake.

Go ahead. Discard that untaken risk and jump. You'll either land softly this time or learn how not to land hard next time. Either way, look before you leap, but leaping is the only way you'll have a shot at soaring.

– 4 –
Drama:
Why most crises are needless

You don't have to be a walking controversy or eccentric to acquire drama in your life. The irony of drama is that most of us create it ourselves. We think too highly of ourselves, and before we know it, our sense of worry is inflated, and anything—any needless or thoughtless comment or act—has been blown out of proportion. As a result, we lose sleep, hair, and even close friends all because of something someone said or did that we allowed to gnaw at us.

Maybe we're not entirely to blame. Sensationalism and controversy sell these days. Just turn on any news station or pick up a magazine about current events or celebrities. Media outlets, Web sites, and even our conversations around the office are laced with drama. It's hard to escape, so no wonder we easily become steeped in it. Throw social networking sites on this fire and you've got combustible emotion. It may seem easier to just watch everything explode so that time can be spent picking up the pieces. At least it's not boring.

One solution? Concern yourself less—much less—with others' opinions of you and you'll soon realize that they probably actually have no substantive opinion of you anyway. We spend a lot of time in life trying to follow rules designed by and imposed by others. Instead of creating an environment, world, or business in which we can thrive, we bend our desires and shelve our dreams for the hope of fitting in.

It's time to chart your own course, critics be darned. By ignoring the words of your critics, you'll soon silence them, and by devoting time and energy to creating the life you want to live—the life full of meaning and passion that you've always dreamed of—you'll be happier and healthier.

Eliminate drama from your life and you'll find

yourself with more time and energy to devote to what matters (or to discovering it). The next time you sense drama creeping into your life, run the other way. Refuse to participate in certain conversations or even to befriend certain people. In order to get the drama out of your life, you'll need to get rid of the situations and steer clear of the characters who help to create it. You won't be missing much; these situations and individuals aren't helping you find your passion. They are distracting you. Your life doesn't need them or the drama they create.

— 5 —
An expensive car: You paid a lot for an hour of enjoyment

In 2010, the average price of a new car in the United States is a whopping $28,400. For many, that may be equivalent to (or more than) your annual salary. For others, it's a reminder of how much it can now cost to get from point A to point B.

Remember: this is just the average price of a new car, incorporating the various makes and models— minivans, a family sedan, that slick sports car that goes very fast and gets you there quickly, and the subcompact economy car. Your own car may have cost twice as much or half as much. Regardless, Americans spend a lot on cars when they don't need to. If you're not passionate about your car, then why devote so much of your income to it when the money could be used toward the discovery or expression of your passion?

I've never had a car payment. Never. I'm not sure how much I have saved each year—or at least freed up to go spend on coffee—but I suspect the amount is significant. I've never had a car payment, because I've never had a new car. Each automobile in my name has been a hand-me-down, something my parents no longer wanted or needed to drive or own, and so it became mine.

Sure, I've lost out on the freedom and chance to choose. Whether it was a white sedan or a charcoal SUV, whatever I've driven was my only option, but I've been happy (enough) behind the wheel. And while rental opportunities or nice friends have given me the chance to drive something that has a higher performance engine or a sexier body, the lust for speed or high-end engineering has never taken hold of me to the extent I want to shell out the money each month such a vehicle would cost.

I have also questioned why I should spend a tidy

sum on something that only provides an hour or two of enjoyment on any given day. We spend much more time in our clothes, our bed, and our homes. Why not spend accordingly?

Expensive cars—or expensive anythings, for that matter—are often purchased simply to let others know that we have the purchasing power to do so. It's known as conspicuous consumption. An expensive automobile may seem important to you now, but it's easily something your life can do without. Get rid of the expensive price tag of a car, and watch your will to care about what others drive decline as well.

What would you do with thousands of extra dollars or a few hundred dollars each month? What could you try? What new risks could you take? Perhaps the key to unlocking your passion is sitting in your driveway.

Five thousand Facebook friends: The weak ties rarely bind

Facebook limits the number of people you're allowed to be "friends" with to around 5,000. There is no precise reason that the company chose this number, but when you reach it, you can no longer accept any new requests. The life of a celebrity must be incredibly taxing with inconveniences like this one.

But maybe Facebook has a point. How many "friends" is too many? Is there a limit to the number of people you can know? Some social theorists insist that 150 is the maximum number of people that an organization can include and still keep a sense of community, authenticity, and meaning. Some churches and offices have kept this in mind and then split into two groups when the 150 benchmark number is reached.

The number is arbitrary, but the meaning is universal: there is a limit to the number of meaningful, personal relationships any one of us can maintain. It's time, then, to focus on the relationships that mean the most and let the others fall by the wayside.

Think of it as the difference between strong and weak ties. The strong ties are those relationships that matter—those friends who will stand beside you on your wedding day or lift your casket when you move on from this life. They are those who will take your calls, spend time with you just doing nothing, and know exactly what to get you for your birthday. They know your families, your pasts, and your dreams. And they support them all.

Weak ties, on the other hand, are people you meet on airplanes, at conferences, or through a similar line of work. The connection is valuable and useful, but it rarely goes deeper than what either party can provide for the other. To be socially balanced, you need a good measure of each, but you should never stake your happiness, livelihood, or importance on the weak connections, no matter how many you have.

Weak connections can get you a new job, but not a real sense of fulfillment that comes from it. Weak ties can help you get noticed, but they do not bring you love. And they can help you find answers to a problem, but probably not the meaning of life. Many of us spend too much time building the weaker network and seeking its approval instead of investing deeply in the strong ties and watching them sustain us our entire life.

Your life doesn't need thousands of weak ties; it needs a handful of strong ones. Get rid of the weak ones that are taking too much time and energy away from allowing you to build a meaningful network of people who deeply care about you and for whom you care.

— 7 —
Stuff from SkyMall:
What happened to your judgment
at 30,000 feet?

It happens every time, as if it's an instinct. We're on our final approach into wherever it is I'm headed and I've packed up my laptop and earphones. If I don't have a book or magazine handy, there's only one thing to look at until I can turn my phone on and check email or send a text message to my wife to let her know I've landed: SkyMall.

For the record, I have never bought anything from SkyMall directly, but I've wanted to. Whether it's something to make my pet's life easier or a clever way to hide a garden hose, SkyMall has a seemingly innovative way to solve every household problem. (By the way, my cat already has it pretty easy and I've never had to hide my garden hose from anyone.)

The problem isn't SkyMall, of course, but rather anything that grabs our attention and tells us to spend money. Maybe it's a daily coupon site that tempts you to buy services you never wanted until you received that morning's email. They're offering 75 percent off belly dancing classes? I never wanted to learn, but now I do! It's so cheap, I'd be a fool not to take these classes!

Many of us end up with too many things that our life doesn't need because we buy all of this stuff. Our houses are full of distracting things precisely because we were tricked into thinking these things were worth getting in the first place, usually because someone simply called our attention to the opportunity to buy them.

The easy thing to do is to eliminate these messages. Our life doesn't need catalogs or emails telling us to buy things we don't need. When we fill our days with these messages, we'll make purchases time and again until someone writes a book and tells us to get rid of all of it. Prevent that from happening by getting rid of the cause, not just the effects.

There is also a bigger lesson to keep in mind here: distractions will creep up more and more often the closer you are to discovering your passion. Just as the urge to thumb through the catalog in the seatback pocket inevitably appears as the plane lands, as soon as you've articulated your passion, lots of things will try to distract you.

Blame it on the cosmos, call it bad karma, or consider it a healthy temptation. Regardless, keep your guard up during such moments. If you have made it to the point where you've nearly discovered your passion, stay on course. Ignore the tempting desire to get distracted, and you'll arrive having finally found what it is that stirs you.

– 8 –
Dishonesty:
There is no such thing as a little lie

My daughter can't talk yet (in a language we can understand), but no doubt once she learns to use words, one of the most challenging parenting lessons will be teaching her what truth is, what lying is, and why you should always tell the truth, no matter who you're talking to.

Of course the old adage reminds us, "If you always tell the truth, you'll never have to remember what you said." Exactly. Dishonesty builds upon itself until eventually we have no option but to unravel the entire whopper and come clean (this is in fact a universal truth that applies to everyone at all times everywhere, outside of Washington, D.C.). We could have saved time, energy, and frustration if we'd just told the truth.

Your life doesn't need dishonesty. Rarely does it stop with one lie. Read any children's book about the subject and you'll see that trying to cover up the bad test score or broken lamp only amounts to more lies and confusion and Mom or Dad is never happy with the outcome. In essence, then, nothing has changed since childhood. What you didn't need in your life then you don't need in your life now. Stop lying in any form—to yourself or to others—and you won't have to keep track of what you've said and to whom you've said it. You'll then spend less time worrying what it was you said and if you'll be found out.

Truth, even as absolute as we'd like to make it, still has a gray area. Because truth can encompass facts and data as well as life lessons and wisdom, it's a big tent under which many ambiguities can hide. What about telling the truth, but not the whole truth? Or what about those things that are true, but not factual (the lessons we learn from childhood stories and fables, for example)? How do we know when we're being completely honest since honesty itself can be defined so many different ways, made up of so many disparate parts? Not to mention the white lies that don't hurt anyone and don't seem to build upon themselves. Telling someone they don't look fat in a certain dress or that someone will find Mister or Miss Right if they just keep trying causes much less harm than the brutal alternative of no-holds-barred honesty. Philosophers and ethicists have written volumes about this concept, but I think we can all benefit by remembering that we can always use less dishonesty in our lives and much more truth. Choose appropriately.

Best of all, when you commit to being honest and getting dishonesty out of your life, you'll begin to be more honest with yourself. This is important to finding your passion. If you don't love something or something doesn't feel right, you needn't lie to yourself that it does, you can simply admit it. You don't want to find yourself down the road several miles when you should never have made that turn to begin with. You'll know if a certain interest or passion really appeals to you. Admit it to yourself when something feels wrong—and when it feels right—and you'll be sure to find that passion that is yours and worth pursuing wholeheartedly.

~ 9 ~
Things you wear once:
It's okay to find yourself in
someone else's pants

Tuxedoes, formal dresses, squirrel costumes, and airplane life vests all have one thing in common: you wear them once for a very specific purpose and then you're done with them. So why is your closet so full of single-use garments?

Maybe it's the part of you that likes to remember. You gaze at the shiny black shoes that match your tux while getting ready for work and very quickly reminisce about the time you danced like crazy at your wedding. You know you will never put those shoes on again, but it's fun—and maybe soothing— to know that you could. Of course, to fit the tux that goes with them you'd also need to lose a few pounds. If there actually were a good reason to get all dressed up, you'd need a bread and water regimen for a few weeks.

And that's why you should rent what needs wearing once—even if it's an annual affair. Finding yourself in someone else's pants—especially someone you've never met—can certainly feel uncomfortable. Embrace that. Or ask a friend (of about the same size and shape) if you could borrow a dress or shoes or a bow tie.

Ultimately, purchasing single-use clothing puts you in an ownership habit, which is what you should be trying to kick. The notion that you have to buy and be in possession of a certain piece of cloth is what your life doesn't need. With ownership comes power, but the rule does not apply to knowing you have a handful of gowns you wore for only a few hours. An uncluttered closet is actually more empowering than a closet stuffed with rarely worn clothing.

Best of all, knowing that you don't have to own it makes you a better shopper, no matter how attractive the sale at the mall seems right now. This lesson also applies to other single-use items. Why fork over the cash for a ladder or a drill if you can borrow one from a neighbor? Identify the things in your life, closet, and garage that you don't need repeatedly. Sell them and use the money on something you need often.

The next time a single-use situation arises, tap into your network and see what can be borrowed. You will build a deeper sense of community, which is an added bonus.

– 10 –
Textbooks: Outdated the moment you bought it

I'm quite certain that my daughter (who is not yet a year old) will never own a textbook. Growing up, I observed thick accounting manuals and philosophy tomes on the bottom shelf of my parents' bookcase in our family room. I never saw them opened, but I knew they were books my parents used in college.

When I entered high school, both the books and my classmates had grown over the summer, and I was thankful to have a locker in between many of my classes so that my backpack didn't weigh me down. Heavy books telling how to solve calculus problems, speak Spanish, and everything I wanted to know about human anatomy made their way to and from school with me each day. I read most of what each textbook contained, answered the questions at the end of each assigned reading section, and toted the book back to class. What a way to learn.

With scads of information available online, many books today aren't even printed on paper (you may in fact be reading this one on a digital reading device). Not only that, since information is updated ever more rapidly, buying an overpriced textbook that conveys a semester's worth of information accurate for no more than a few years can become nearly unthinkable. What is more, with much learning happening in a decentralized manner where there is no "expert," students read many sources for the information they need to complete a term paper or pass an exam. Those who buy a textbook rarely keep them. And neither should you.

It's okay to keep some things from college, but not many (more about that later), and certainly not textbooks. If you want to cull your bookshelf, start there. If you really need the info, you'll be able to find it online, at the library, or from a smaller book.

If you know that any book—not just a textbook—is outdated, your life doesn't need it.

Textbooks were not always so expensive, but the days of shelling out $100 for something you may barely open over the course of a few months may soon be gone. One can only hope. It will save me a fortune on my daughter's education.

$-11-$
Bad wine:
It's time to find a drink you love

Some of the most iconic characters of our time, both real and imaginary, found one thing they loved and didn't waver. President Reagan always kept a bowl of jelly beans handy for guests. Einstein wore that same black suit and tie every day. James Bond always drank a martini, shaken. Perhaps you can learn from them.

Variety is certainly the spice of life, but be honest with yourself. Do you really care about spice? If you don't, then find your one thing and stick with it. Case in point: If you enjoy social drinking, what's your drink of choice? Sure, it may depend on the menu, but knowing what it is you want to order and what you like saves time when you step up to the bar. You don't want to spit out your drink all over your boyfriend's parents the first time you meet them. And you don't want to be sick later when you realize the drink didn't sit well on your stomach.

Finding your favorite cocktail or wine may require experiments, but once you find it, stick with it. Don't settle for anything less. Don't drink something just because it is free. Don't waste your time or palate on something you don't like when you know what you love.

One of the best anecdotes on this subject comes from Yvon Chouinard, founder of the Patagonia apparel company. He tells that once he was at a house party and the wine being served was not to his liking. Rather than suffer through the rest of the glass, he excused himself to the restroom and poured out the contents. He would rather throw away bad wine than put it into his body.

Once you find what it is you like to drink—whether it's a pinot noir or a screwdriver—stick with it. The same thing applies when you discover your passion. Don't waste time on pursuits that distract you from living it out. Don't be anything less than completely committed.

‒ 12 ‒
Pictures that don't mean anything: Defining sentiment for yourself

As soon as we move into a new place, we feel compelled to put stuff on the wall. There is something about our human condition that forces us to make sure a poster, a piece of art, a tapestry, or a photograph hangs on a wall. Blankness is boring.

Every retail store sells art. Sure, it is produced in a factory, but it is still color on canvas. And it can be yours for one low price! Best of all, no matter the store you visit, you can find the same piece anywhere across the country. This isn't a pretty picture. If blankness is boring, sameness is nauseating. Case in point: after you buy the artwork, you pay your friend a visit and notice the same thing hanging on her wall. What you thought was catchy and unique is merely mainstream and popular. It's time you discarded pictures that don't mean anything to you. Wall and shelf space are finite. Don't fill them with art that doesn't stir you or serve as a reminder of your life's purpose.

Today's cameras and editing software can make nearly anyone a good photographer (but to be a great photographer still requires skill and training). For a small investment, you can quickly obtain prints of loved ones and places you've visited for your wall, which is much better than a poster that reminds you of an errand to the store.

Local art is also easier to find. You don't have to be an art history major or even passed art appreciation to find something you like. As long as it stirs something noble within you, it's a piece of art with a great purpose. Look around your local community: visit a coffee shop, go to a gallery opening, or take a stroll at the library. You are bound to find something produced by hand by someone nearby. Whatever you decide to own—whether it's a vase, a painting, or a sculpture—it will be a much better conversation starter than the thing that came in a box that everyone else has in his living room.

This is why it is important not to be a conformer. Many rules are worth breaking, especially those imposed upon you arbitrarily (selling drugs or driving way too fast does not fit the category). Who says that you have to take wedding pictures like everyone else? Who says you can't have original artwork in every room in your house? These may seem to be unwritten rules, but you can safely break them.

Find a piece of art or a picture that inspires you, or create your own. Perhaps in their creation you will find a new and exciting passion worth exploring further, filling your life with passion and beauty instead of mass-produced monotony.

– 13 –
Unpassionate activism:
Find your cause and dive in

All around the world, well-meaning individuals are falling prey to an epidemic: we've got cause fatigue. I know. Poor us. In trying to help real people with real problems, we ourselves become our own victims. Our purse strings and heartstrings are tugged and yanked a thousand different directions, from the cause of the moment to the perennial issues of hunger and poverty. We give in and cry uncle, tossing $20 to this friend and that one. Doing so raises small amounts of money and attention and quickly, but very few of us end up exploring the issues that make us want to invest our wholehearted time and energy.

Perhaps I am to blame. After all, I created and run a company that tells people how to get involved with one new cause each weekday. We have been doing this for four years. Whether the issue is the environment, literacy, community, or wildlife, Cool People Care has been attracting an audience of do-gooders interested in small, tangible actions that can be taken to improve the world.

We never meant for the activism to end with small steps. The idea was to showcase needs and causes, entice the reader to try a small action to find his niche, and then push him into the local community to find an organization nearby working on the issue directly. The person could then team up with the local nonprofit and become a regular volunteer, donor, or board member. The goal was and is to create new advocates willing to tell others about an issue of great importance to them.

It's okay if your activism starts small, but it shouldn't stay small. Your life doesn't need you to be unpassionate about causes. You need to find the one or two things you want to change and jump in with both feet. Wading along the shoreline is fun, but you should plan to swim the deep end with all your time and talents. Once you do, other issues that are important will give way to your focus.

Passionate activists and donors are the best ones a nonprofit can find. When someone is willing to tell her network—friends, family, colleagues—about a certain cause, the nonprofit saves money and time. Best of all, that advocate can make a more personal and relevant appeal, increasing the amount of time or money given. Therefore, when you become passionate and active about a particular cause, exciting your community about it will create an exponential return in action and voluntarism. Serving as head cheerleader, you will be able to motivate people in a unique and relevant way and connect more people to the cause than ever before. Your deep and singular activism is important for the issue you care deeply about, because without you, it could struggle or founder.

Find your cause and dive in.

– 14 –
More than one junk drawer: One is enough

I've tried many times to get rid of my junk drawer, that one drawer that seems to house everything that doesn't have a place. Much as I have tried, I have realized it will never happen. I'll always need somewhere to put everything that doesn't belong somewhere else. So I have concluded that it's okay to have one junk drawer, but no more. The minute you start having more than one place for things that don't have a place, you're missing the point and just being lazy. The beauty of a junk drawer is that it can still be organized. You can still have a tray or small boxes or compartments for pens and pins and whatever you decide belongs there.

Here is another rule for junk drawers: you have to be able to remember what's in there. If you forget what's in there or you haven't used it in so long you don't even know that you own it, your life doesn't need it. Get rid of it or put it where it belongs. The litmus test for whether your life needs something is just this: do you even know you own it? How long would it take you to make a list of everything you own? Could you even do it? What if whatever didn't make the list had to be tossed out? Would you be willing to start making such a list?

Chances are, there are lots of things your life doesn't need simply because you don't even know you have them. Sometimes, the junk drawer is the last stop for an item before it's thrown or given away. This is okay—it signals progress that you are whittling down what your life doesn't need.

Movements have long been afoot to inspire people to simplify their lives by challenging them to get by on only 100 things in their homes or 10 items in their wardrobe. The number doesn't matter so much as the focus on how much is too much. Even if you don't pare your household items down to exactly

100, the exercise itself will reveal how many things you own and what you really don't need.

So, keep a junk drawer. Keep things in it that you are always looking for. Take stock of it once a year and clear out the items you don't need.

― 15 ―
Unused suitcases:
The world really is your oyster

I own too many suitcases. There—I said it. Each one seems to have its purpose, based on where I'm going, how long I'm staying, with whom I'm traveling, and how I'm getting there. Sure, I could cull the inventory, but the bigger point is this: suitcases are meant to be used.

I'm guessing you own a few suitcases yourself. Maybe you bought a giant one for your two-week trip to Europe, or you found a great deal on a smaller bag you just had to have. Whatever the occasion, if you're not using a suitcase, you need to get rid of it. It sits there, empty, taking up space.

Better yet, you could use it. You could travel. Get your passport updated and see the world. Buy a ticket to anywhere and learn something about a place you've never visited. Explore a new country and culture. Learn part of a language. See what it's like to be away from the comforts and routine of home.

Some people love traveling and others just seem to tolerate it. Traveling for pleasure is much better than trips you have to take somewhere for business, but the benefits can be the same regardless of motive. Going somewhere gives you the opportunity to explore. Once you navigate the downtown core of a new city, for example, examining your own heart and past and your goals may not seem so scary.

Before you get rid of your suitcases, fill them up and hit the road. Give one a few scuffs and dents and open up a whole new world. Keep a journal of what you see and learn and don't be afraid to ask yourself difficult questions about the kind of person you want to be. Moving around could help you to move on, or move forward. Inertia is a scientific law; there is no getting around it. You need a great deal of resolve to get moving, but once in motion, you can continue your path of progress toward self-discovery and personal fulfillment.

– 16 –

Fraternity pins:
College is over. Move on

It's okay to act as if you're still in college when you have been an alumnus for only a year. Well, maybe it's not okay, but at least it's excusable. You don't get the same pass when you have been out of school for nearly a decade.

You can still cheer for your alma mater when they play football or talk up your former stomping ground when your niece is filling out college applications. But if you still wear fraternity T-shirts or if the best days of your life were when you sometimes overslept for your 8:00 a.m. psych class, it's time to move on.

No one doubts that college can be formative, for better or worse. You learn skills and meet people who will help you the rest of your life. Extracurricular experiences can be as valuable as those inside the classroom, setting you forever on a different pathway toward your life's goals and dreams. But come graduation, it is time to close a chapter of your life and begin another.

Most of us have similar ties, whether or not we belonged to sorority or fraternity clubs. Sorority T-shirts are okay to wear when going jogging or washing the car; wearing them to get coffee or go shopping probably isn't. Walking down memory lane when friends are in town is fine; comparing everything at your new job to your time on campus is not. No one wants to take away your memories, but the world after college isn't a Pi Kappa Phi semi-formal.

The past is valuable. It teaches plenty of lessons through experience that shape both the present and the future. But no one was meant to live there. Wearing a certain shirt every now and then doesn't lock you to the past, but it may keep you tethered more than you realize. Live in the present and dream about tomorrow, with the past guiding you as a healthy reminder of how things can turn out. But don't be so tied to it that you are kept from moving forward to create your own future. Your life doesn't need to be trapped in yesterday. It needs to be lived today.

Whether it's college memorabilia, high school notebooks, or lots of paperwork from a past job, your life doesn't need so many tangible reminders of what took place so long ago. Taking stock of the things you own which pin you to the past and prohibit you from moving forward and discovering the life you were meant to live is a healthy exercise that could reveal to you new goals, horizons, and opportunities. Get rid of something that's chaining you to the past and start living for tomorrow, today.

– 17 –
Empty journals:
Get it write

B arbara Walters once said her only regret was that she didn't keep a diary. That's a heavy statement coming from someone who has met nearly every influential person of the last half a century. Some of us might care to know what a TV personality thinks of the behavior of former heads of state when the cameras are off or what Hollywood royalty does after the interview. We might also want to know how a woman so successful was able to rise to the top. Any insight into the daily discipline of a successful person could be a great motivator for the rest of us looking to do great things with our one, passionate life.

I'm the king of starting journals. I get a shiny new one, ready for my pen to fill its pages with beautiful blue ink. I get excited enough to write a few pages on the first day. I'll keep it up the fol-lowing day and I may even get half a dozen entries complete before journaling seems like the last thing I want to do (in the morning or evening). I'm afraid I can offer little advice about how to keep at it with a journal, but I do know you need an outlet for writing down all the thoughts and emotions you have in your head and heart each day. My wife has kept a private journal for years. Upon her death, I am (or the near-est surviving relative is) to incinerate all of her jour-nals without reading them. Even if the audience is a single person (you and you alone), the act of writing down your thoughts, feelings, hopes, and dreams is an important one. Whether you intend to share your diary with the world or keep it under lock and key, getting in the habit of writing one can be truly trans-formative.

Whether I type on my computer and publish all (or some of it) in a blog post or book, or whether I scribble an idea on a spare notepad, I have found that giving voice to my thoughts and putting into words my feelings is a discipline worth keeping, especially as it relates to discovering who I am and learning what it is I love. If it was important enough to write down, maybe it's important enough to explore a bit further.

Go to the store and get an empty journal and begin to fill it up. The journal is entirely yours and there are no rules other than that it can't stay blank. Scribble down song lyrics that inspire you or keep a record of quotations that motivate you. Draw pictures. Paste in cartoons. Keep a list of your goals, hopes, and dreams. Read over them as often as you can and feel the rush of excitement that only comes with having great and lofty ambitions.

What you write today may seem bland and uninspiring, but it may be the best sort of motivation when you read it again in a month's time. You could become your own best inspiration, but only if you write it down.

– 18 –
The latest digital toy:
Why first is rarely best

New releases—whether we're talking about movies or music players—are exciting. Lots of TV commercials and advertising tout them and when they get here, it is easy to feel like we're missing out if we don't own them. Waiting, however, is generally smarter. Our lives do not need the latest anything, especially if it's the first generation of a new thing. My rule of thumb is never to buy the first generation of a new product and to buy the latest only when mine is at least three generations older.

I don't know how many times the iPod has been improved upon. Just when it seems as if they've made the perfect one, out comes a newer version that does one or two things differently. What we're (seemingly) left with is an obsolete device that does lots of things well except for the one or two things that the new one does. We end up with buyer's remorse and we fume at our own impatience.

In reality, the device is probably not obsolete, at least not yet. What we have—even if it's been improved upon—still works just fine. Upgrades are usually a tech company's strategy to ensure that their products keep selling. If you were to buy a new TV, car, or phone only when you needed one, you would spend less money, and the companies who provide the products would make less of a profit. Filling the airwaves and your ears with promises of all the new and better things their gadget can do is a brilliant marketing move. From their perspective, I suppose it makes sense. If the company doesn't make a profit, it goes broke, and employees lose their jobs.

Your life, however, doesn't need the latest new digital toy. Your current digital toy works well enough. Besides, the first version of something is rarely ready for primetime. The first version of this book wasn't worth reading, and the first phones with access to the Internet weren't nearly as good as what almost every phone is capable of today.

Likewise, when something new comes out and launches amid much fanfare, you may have to wait in line for it. This is valuable time you can never get back. Let others wait in line and buy the phones or music players that still need the kinks worked out. If you're willing to wait, you'll get a better (and often cheaper) version. No matter how strong and over-whelming your impatience may be, it's not worth sacrificing your passion for or putting the search for your passion on hold. Waiting to purchase a status symbol may also help you build patience, a key trait that may ultimately help you find and live your passion.

Focus on your passion. It's much more important than owning the latest iPod.

– 19 –
Bottled water: Why pay $3 for something that costs 16 cents?

Most of the things you eliminate from your life will make you a better inhabitant of the planet. The less you consume, the more you conserve for others. The old triad of "reduce, reuse, recycle" is ordered that way for a reason, placed in perfect sequence for its benefit to nature. When you decrease consumption, you curb waste and pollution. If going green is your motivation for simplifying your life, have at it. It's a noble pursuit; one I wholeheartedly embrace.

You'll find that avoiding bottled water offers many benefits in addition to cleaning up the good Earth. You'll save money and time and you'll be able to better focus on finding what it is you love doing. Sure—if you're in dire need of a drink and you've got no other option than to buy a bottle of water or die, I highly recommend that you choose the water. Buying it to consume at home, however, with the thought that, unlike tap water, it is pure, is money down the drain. Literally. The amount of water that comes in bottles for 3 dollars can be had for 16 cents from your tap. Get rid of the bottled stuff and watch your bank account grow.

Although advances in plastics have been made, by swearing off bottled water entirely, you'll be decreasing the amount of plastic needed to bottle it all. The entire process of manufacturing and shipping bottled water requires a hefty amount of oil. When the price of oil increases, so does everything that uses it. Though bottled water may cost 3 dollars today, it will eventually cost more.

And, in developed countries, what comes out of your tap is perfectly fine to drink. If you're feeling a bit paranoid, purchase a filter that attaches to your faucet. Even with the initial cost of a filter and pitcher, you'll still save money in the long run. That's hard-earned cash that you can use for whatever you want (except something from SkyMall).

Once you're willing to eschew the bottled water, you will probably find a slew of other things that can go by the wayside—things that can be replaced with a cheaper and eco-friendly alternative. For an entire list of ideas, visit CoolPeopleCare.org.

– 20 –
Boring hobbies:
If it doesn't excite you, don't do it

L ots of people spend time doing things they hate, but these activities are not limited to just a job. Many people spend time and focus on things outside of work—hobbies, volunteer activities, and other recreational pursuits—that they would rather avoid. One hopes that some of what they do is enjoyable or exciting, but many people end up hating these extra activities, often because they feel obligated for one reason or another. Maybe you are invited somewhere and feel that you need to attend, out of obligation to a friend or family member. Maybe you join a sports league or gym and keep making yourself go because you'll hate yourself if you don't and you tell your-self that it's somehow good for you. Or maybe you volunteer somewhere but are beginning to grow tired of the mission, the organization, or the other people lending a hand.

You could force yourself to continue onward, slogging through another early morning or late evening, but very soon that feeling of obligation will turn into a feeling of resentment. Resentment will then grow into revulsion, and revulsion is good for no one. Your life doesn't need a boring hobby or another obligation that makes you cringe.

In these situations, you need to learn the word "no." When someone asks you to help out with something you're not passionate or excited about, you should politely turn down the offer. When you see a membership discount at the fitness center, even though you'll either never go or loathe going, you need to keep moving and keep your money in your pocket. Be honest with yourself and others about what you like—and what you don't enjoy. Those you turn down will appreciate your honesty and only approach you in the future with ideas that are in line with your values or interests. This means that the opportunities that present themselves will be better suited to you and worth looking into. You'll decrease the amount of hobby-related "spam" in your life, freeing up time and resources for interests that truly speak to you.

People I have met who seem to really be making an impact in their local communities or who have found an after-hours endeavor they are really passionate about decline anything that's not aligned with what they enjoy doing. The goal should never be to fill your calendar with commitments; it should be to commit to the things that matter and plan everything else around them. Doing so will make you a happier person and a better community advocate.

What activities seem boring to you? What doesn't excite you? What do you hate attending? What meetings are wastes of time or a drain on your resources? If you don't look forward to something, it's time for you to bow out of the commitment. Talk to the person in charge and let him know that you will be moving on to another activity. Spend time looking around your community for extracurricular activities that you are excited about. Ask friends how they spend their free time and explore whether their interests are a match with yours.

You'll know when you find the thing that's right for you. When you enjoy it, go all out. Your passion will begin to show itself, and you will be happier and more interested as a result.

− 21 −

T-shirts that serve as proof of something: No one cares where you were last night

T-shirts and sweatshirts are easy to emboss and have become a staple in the wardrobes of many people. People like to buy them for hundreds of reasons. I should know this—Cool People Care decorates thousands of T-shirts for charitable causes every year.

At some point, however, you can acquire too many T-shirts. Sooner or later, those shirts you got for running the Timbuktu cross-country three-miler or surviving the ascent of Pikes Peak go unworn, stacking up and filling your dressers and closets with no hope of seeing the light of day. Warm and fuzzy memories may be attached to that cotton shirt, but your life doesn't need wearable proof that you were there.

You'll never wear them to work, which is where you spend most of your time. You may think of throwing one on when you get home at the end of the day to have something to sleep in. But how many people will see the shirt and acknowledge your greatness for having been at a certain place at a certain time? Maybe you wear these shirts to the gym or when working in the yard. While apropos, few people spend a lot of time at these activities, again decreasing the true impact of the shirt and why you bought it.

If you're curious about whether or not you have too many shirts, keep track of how many you wear this month. If you only wear a few during the course of several weeks, there is no reason to have several dozen. Make the hard decision to pare down your number of shirts immediately. Once you take a stack of shirts and donate them to a shelter or secondhand store, you'll find that you don't miss them. Letting them go will teach you that you no longer need so many shirts, especially those that commemorate some kind of event.

Before you spend money at an event for a shirt, either commit to getting rid of an old shirt, or stop this practice altogether. Colleges make shirts for every football game and fraternity party. Nostalgia is great, except when it comes at the expense of your future plans. Minimize or eliminate T-shirts and sweatshirts altogether and you'll find more money in your hand and more room in your closet. Use both wisely.

– 22 –
Analog versions of digital stuff: Let technology work for you

With comprehension of the latest in digital gadgetry, there comes a time when we can replace analog or "real world" versions of things with their digital equivalent. In less than a decade, we've gone from taking pictures with real film to filling cameras, computers, and Facebook pages with digital memories. Millions of digital books are now sold every year. Important documents can be scanned and stored, nearly immune from the accidents and disasters that can destroy important papers. What in your life can be made digital, allowing you to eliminate the nondigital versions from your life?

Most user guides to software are available online. Coupons can be emailed to you each day. Home movies can be viewed over the Internet. Inventory systems, checklists, financial statements, bills, and receipts never need to be printed and held in your hand again. By keeping these parts of your everyday life online, you'll reduce clutter, save time and money, and see how easy it is to let technology work for you.

Begin keeping a list tomorrow of everything you come across that can be digitized. Remove your name from junk mail and catalog lists (view the products online). Buy music and rent movies online. Send pictures of your kids to relatives and friends by email and keep everything in online storage. Enjoy the speed of technology and use the extra time to do something you love and find important.

Advances in search technology and online storage continue to improve. Not only will you save space, but you will also find what you're looking for much more quickly. No longer will you be confused about where you put a photo album. With a few clicks, you can easily locate pictures and videos and show everything to loved ones. Digital collections are also better than prints; they never fade and are always where you can find them.

Once you get the knack of it, it will feel much more natural and you can begin to experiment with other tasks that can be done digitally. Lots of progress has been made in the digital world in a short time, and the rate of progress doesn't appear to be slowing. Hop on board and enjoy the ride.

— 23 —
Instruction manuals:
Learn something intimately

Everything comes with an instruction manual. Very few of us actually read them. Some manuals have seemed to shorten over the years and their parts and procedures become more commonplace and easier to operate. Most TVs and computers nowadays only require you to open the box, plug them in, and turn them on. Programming them, of course, is another matter entirely.

I have done my best to save every instruction manual, whether it's for a blender or a barstool. But what if something breaks? What if I need to take it apart and reassemble it? What if something needs rewiring, or reconfiguring, or replacing? I don't do so well at getting rid of the manual once I no longer have the item. I was cleaning out some shelves one day and found an instruction manual for a coffee maker I hadn't seen in five years.

You can toss your instruction manuals (many are online and available for download if you really need them), but there is another how-to that you should pursue: the need to know the inner workings of a device, particularly if it is electronic. You don't need to learn how all of your laptops actually operate, but taking time to learn more about them other than how to email a friend or watch an online video is time well spent. Even being able to diagnose minor computer problems will save you time and money on customer support.

The need to know isn't limited to the tech world; most furniture comes with some kind of assembly kit. Knowing how to assemble a desk will do won-ders for the analytical and problem-solving parts of your brain. You needn't toss out the manual as soon as you open the box; the idea here is to pay close attention to see how it all fits together as you're as-sembling it.

Best of all, if you limit yourself to owning only the things that you understand thoroughly, you'll get rid of a lot of things in your life you don't care to know about. Learning a software program, a skill, a trade, or a hobby by heart will enable you to commit to those things you truly love and can even build a passion around.

It's easy today to know a little about a lot. The entire world is at our fingertips and with a few clicks of the mouse we can find exactly what we're looking for. This is a fantastic advance in technology, but we can end up not knowing anything deeply. How can you truly find your passion if you only know a little about a lot but not a lot about anything? Spend time learning something deeply, inside and out—whether it's how to repair your computer or how to put together a swingset for your child. The more you know about it, the more you can chase your passion.

Your life shouldn't have to depend on instruction manuals. Do you know anything intimately?

— 24 —

Tax returns older than seven years: Knowing when the window has closed

The rule of thumb is that there is no reason to keep tax returns that are older than seven years. Once you hit that magic anniversary, your entire office or family can have a shredding party and commemorate how little money you used to have. The seven-year mark is one that is suggested by the IRS and most state governments, for questions about your earnings or if there is an audit.

Whether or not you actually throw a party on the seven-year anniversary, the mark should be recognized as a clear signal: if one of the largest bureaucracies of government isn't interested in it, you needn't hang on to it. Extend the time frame to a decade if you like or if you're a hopeless romantic for that return you completed with pencils and calculator in only 15 hours way back in 2001.

The seven-year rule can be applied to many of your dreams. Dream all you want, but letting go of that old flame or high school sweetheart could do wonders for your peace of mind. If you haven't spoken in seven years, forget about it. She has moved on. So should you. After seven years, have you made any progress in realizing your dream? If there has been no progress whatsoever, give it up. Spend time on a new dream. Out of the shattered rubble of unfulfilled dreams a beautiful new one can emerge. Failure can be celebrated. It certainly wasn't your goal, but learning from situations and dreams that didn't pan out is a great silver lining. Some of the best entrepreneurs and inventors didn't succeed on their first try. Edison's famous efforts to find a workable filament for the incandescent lightbulb reportedly required more than a thousand attempts.

The seven-year mark is just a good and convenient rule of thumb; it's certainly not gospel. It may take you a year to realize that a relationship is going nowhere. It may take ten years to discover that your business should shut its doors. Don't be afraid to ask yourself whether or not something is working, and what should be eliminated from your life to free you for better and nobler pursuits. Your life doesn't need stagnant dreams that have produced no value or benefit for seven years.

Getting rid of the many kinds of "tax returns" after seven years takes a bit of faith. The temptation to keep hanging on is very great, and your heart will dare you to hold out hope. But you need to be ruthless. If you keep hanging on, you'll never have the open hand you need to grasp the next thing. Hold these memories and feelings delicately in the palm of your hand. Don't grip them tightly. You'll find out that you can hold much more with an open palm than a closed fist. Let circumstance take away that which you don't need and give you what you desperately want. Be willing to say goodbye to opportunities that are older than seven years and watch for all the new opportunities you will be able to greet with a hello.

– 25 –
Anything belonging to an ex:
Love in the now

O ne of the first things I did when I got engaged (other than call family and friends to tell them the exciting news) was to get rid of anything ever given me by an ex-girlfriend. Old letters and movie ticket stubs composed the bulk of it, so the task was simply to dump things from a shoebox into a re-cycling bin. When I got engaged, that was it—the old romance was now a permanent relic of the past. Therefore, there was no reason to keep a tape that someone had given me with all of "our" songs. I had moved on. Officially.

Whether or not you're married or engaged, your life doesn't need anything that an ex gave you. Old T-shirts, souvenirs, or stuffed animals can all be donated or thrown away. While keeping a small teddy bear in your closet may seem harmless, owning something that no longer carries with it the same powerful emotional meaning is futile and takes up space and attention that could be occupied by something that matters.

If an ex gave it to you, it was given during a happy time, when feelings of love and hope were at their highest. As long as the relationship was intact, rereading the letter or sleeping next to the stuffed animal increased those feelings and made them more real in the absence of the other person. But if the relationship has ended and the feelings have disappeared, why keep the items that symbolized both? What you now own is a cheaply and mass produced toy.

Keeping these things may not take up a lot of space, but knowing that you have them could be preventing you in some way from moving on. Being linked to the past may prevent you—however subtly—from embracing the present. You may be less likely to want to meet someone new, to trust someone fully, or to explore a deeper relationship with anyone. It may seem as though I'm putting too much emphasis on a love note or a bracelet, but if these items stir deep emotion within you, they may end up paralyzing you. If you are tied to remembering an idealistic past, you may find yourself unable to see what's really before you.

What would happen if you got rid of everything an ex gave you? Would it free you up emotionally? Would you feel freer than ever, willing to take new risks to find someone you love? You'll never know until you try. You can still be friends with your ex; just don't keep everything you ever received. Reminisce from time to time, but be as free and open as you can for the next great relationship.

Unbatched errands:
Planning ahead pays

Most people hate running errands, but they love to go shopping. That's because errands seem like necessary evils or tiresome chores. Visiting the Department of Motor Vehicles or running out for pet food isn't nearly as fun as seeing the latest dresses at the mall or catching a movie with some friends.

One of the main reasons people hate errands is that the need to run them occurs so frequently. Big box retailers have tried to simplify things by offering thousands of items under a single roof so we all can get as many things as needed in one place. This is a convenience, but there still comes the need for a specific grocery item from a certain supermarket, or that pair of ankle-support running shoes from a particular shoe store. You're probably scared to do the math for how much time you spend hurrying to and fro, and sitting in your car waiting on traffic. You cringe at the thought of having to leave your house on the weekend to get one more thing that you need by Monday.

The solution is an easy one: batch your errands. If you need to go to the post office, the grocery store, and the photomart, plan your trip so that you take care of all three errands in one outing. In the time it takes to put your shoes on and pull out of your drive the second and third time in a single day, you could have completed one of the errands. Certain emergencies arise, but batching your errands will save you time (and gas). Waiting until the end of the week to buy stamps and mail your packages means standing in line only once that week. Following up the trip with a visit to the dry cleaners (it's probably on the same street) will eliminate an entire trip.

Anything that saves you time or money is worth looking into, especially since it will save precious resources to spend on what you really love—that which you really do want in your life. Batching your errands will also save you many headaches.

What can you accomplish on your way home from work? Is there a neighbor or co-worker you can divide errands with, sharing the task? With a little creativity, you can easily lessen the burden of errands, giving you back several hours a week, time you can use to pursue your passion.

− 27 −
Seasonal dishes:
Those Santa cups are ugly

What is the people-to-plate ratio in your house? 1:8? 1:25? Either way, an obsession with dinnerware isn't good for anyone. Couple that obsession with plates and mugs that are decorated for every holiday or milestone from New Year's to Christmas and you can soon expect your pantry to be full of things to put food on, that is, if you still have any space in the pantry for the food.

Unless part of your job or passion is hosting lavishly themed dinner parties, you don't need more than one set of dishes. And if only three people inhabit your house and you own a dishwasher, more than a dozen mugs, and fifty forks and knives, you're going overboard. Be honest with yourself: if people leave your house after dinner and compliment you on the silverware instead of the wine or the main course, you're focusing on the wrong thing.

Plates and spoons are a means to an end. They don't add any more taste or nutritional value to the food. And as long as they don't detract from either, you are better off not worrying about them. Find some that work and move on. If you lose or break one, replace it. That about sums it up.

The same can be said for decorations. Unless you're very passionate about holidays and host the best party on the block, you can also forget having decorations for every season. Something on the door or your mailbox more than covers your neighborly obligation to get in the spirit of Halloween or Valentine's Day. No one is forcing you to buy heart-shaped wine goblets or pink pencils. Save your money and your time.

Sure, fancy Christmas lights can be festive, but unless you're trying to win the lights contest, skip the hassle. Fitting in has its perks, but they are few and far between. Let your neighbor know that while he was tacking lights to his roof, you were inside learning how to make the perfect cup of hot chocolate or planning your new business.

After all, decorations are merely icing. They are distractions. Spending time making things look pretty in your life, without spending time and resources to discover meaning for your life, is futile and irrelevant. Your passion lies deep within. If you haven't been able to design the blueprint for your dream house, why are you spending time purchasing the window dressing?

Give priority to finding your passion, and you'll find something more entertaining than a giant inflatable snow globe for your front yard.

– 28 –
Gadgets that only do one thing: It's okay to multitask

In this day and age, if you have a phone or a music player that is only a phone or a music player, you're in rare company. Phones now take pictures, offer access to the Internet, serve as a video game player, and—play music. Technology imitates life in that everything does everything, all at once. If you thought you were the king or queen of multitasking, just wait until the next shiny new cell phone is announced.

Why then, would you own something that only does one thing? You certainly want to avoid the temptation to bring home the latest gadget as soon as it is announced, but once something has been proven capable, your life doesn't need a stack of digital tools that only do one thing. They take up too much space and you waste too much time switching back and forth from each gadget just to accomplish one task.

No matter how connected you are, however, the versatility of digital gadgets suggests a tactic that can apply to the rest of your life: why not multitask as much as possible, as long as you're not sacrificing quality for speed? Teenagers are the masters of this strategy. Walk into a young person's room and you will find him playing video games, talking on the phone, sending a text message, chatting online, watching TV, and writing a report. Ask him what he's up to and he'll tell you, "Doing homework."

Any news station does the same thing. At any given point in the day, you'll see a talking head, a live video of a late-breaking story, a weather bar on the left side of the screen, a scrolling news ticker across the bottom, and stock quotes in a corner. Welcome to our world, where everything is happening at once.

It's time you played along, especially with mundane tasks. You may need to ease into this discipline, but learning to make phone calls while folding clothes, carrying a book to read while waiting in line, sending short emails when you find five minutes of downtime, and listening to the day's news while making dinner will save you time that is often desperately needed for seeking your passion.

It is important not to sacrifice quality time or cautious behavior. You don't want to read a magazine while your child is sharing a problem with you, and you don't want to do your makeup while driving to work. Find those tasks in your life that fit well with one another and watch the extra minutes, or even hours, in your life begin to grow.

– 29 –
Regret:
Carpe diem

Learn from failure. Celebrate it. Learning what you did wrong or what led to lackluster results will help you the next time you venture out and try something new. What you shouldn't do is to sit and sulk over what could have been. Your life doesn't have time for regret.

It's always okay to sit and innocently wonder about what could have taken place, but the minute wishful thinking turns into regret or remorse, it's time to stop. Regret is unproductive. No one can turn back time, and though aging movie stars may not realize it, plastic surgery is only skin deep. No matter how hard you try, and how great you armchair quarterback the foiled play, you'll never be able to implement it. There is no going back for another try because the game was called for rain. This is not sandlot baseball. It's life. Learn and move on.

Usually, when some celebrity is asked if she has any regrets about a certain time in her life, the answer is an emphatic, "No." While admirable, I wonder if celebrities are telling the truth. If they are, good for them. I respect that they seem to live their lives with no regrets, but having no regrets is something that is always easier to say in response to an interview question than it is to live out.

If you were in the hot seat, being interviewed for the TV news or a magazine, what would you say? Examine your life and your past and see if there truly is something you're holding on to, something that you still hold out hope for that is improbable or impossible. If so, let it go. You have my permission.

Now, move on to the present, and make the best decisions you can so that you not only have no time for regret, but your life is so well lived that it creates none.

– 30 –
Unknown relatives:
Find out where you came from

I'm not sure why, but once I began college, whenever I visited my grandparents, I would ask them to tell me about their lives in youth. I'd take meticulous notes in a journal on every word they said. Perhaps motivating me was Bruce Northam, author of Globetrotter Dogma, who wrote, "When grandparents die, libraries burn." The point? Get the stories from these people, because when they disappear, so do their stories.

I learned how and why and when my great-great-grandparents moved from Ohio. I caught a glimmer of what it must have been like to get married at sixteen, have eight kids, and work an industrial factory job. I learned about cousins I barely knew, places I have never visited, and ways of life I could never imagine. My grandmother's stories became increasingly valuable to me once she began to be able to remember less, and even more so once she had passed away. I had gotten to know her better, and learned a lot about myself.

That's what happens when we get to know family. No matter how distant they may seem, the convenience of technology and the ease of travel makes family reunions and updates easier than ever. The excuse of ignorance becomes less and less valid. Even if you haven't known someone since you were a child, there is no reason you can't get to know them now.

By discovering and developing relationships with family members, you'll learn about yourself, too. You'll learn where you came from, how people can view the same person very differently, and what it is that unites seemingly different people. You may also find an opportunity to explore your passion. Turning inward—toward your own family—can help open an entirely new world.

What relative do you barely know? Who have you not seen in ages? Who could use a call or email from you, even if it's not a major holiday? Rekindle a familial relationship today and watch your world expand. Your life doesn't need your relatives to be strangers.

– 31 –
Unvoiced love:
Say what you feel

The feeling is there. It's in your heart and on the tip of your tongue. Sure, it's risky and you may look foolish, but you need to say how you feel. Otherwise, how else will the person know? Go ahead. Say it. Tell them you love them. Your life doesn't need repressed feelings. Get it out there and see what happens.

When I was in second grade, I fell in love. It was a new emotion to me, and all I had to go on was what I'd seen on TV. Every time someone on TV fell in love, they wrote a love letter. That seemed like a good plan.

I could keep my feelings bottled no longer, so I spent an entire evening crafting a love letter to the object of my affection. After what seemed like hours of work, I produced a document that accurately conveyed the new and intense emotions happening in my heart. It read:

Dear Jenny,
You are beautiful. I like you.
Love, Sam

Those ten words contained everything I'd ever wanted to say to Jenny. With the note completed, I folded it and placed it in my backpack and waited until school the next day until I could give it to Jenny. I imagined that once she read it, she would feel the same and want to marry me on the spot. That was a tall order for a second-grader, but I was in love and ready to commit. I'd talk to my parents later and go ask her dad for his blessing.

When I arrived at school the next day, Jenny was nowhere to be found. I hoped she was okay—this was my fiancée-to-be we were talking about. Nearly heartbroken, I would have to wait another day to share my love.

Later that day, the teacher announced that it was time to clean out our desks. Second-graders seldom exhibit a high level of organizational skill, so from time to time there is a need for the entire class to clean up and straighten books, craft supplies, and educational games.

Since Jenny was not present to clean up her desk, the teacher asked for volunteers. I stepped up—the young humanitarian that I was becoming—mainly because I figured the perfect place to put the note would be in her school supply box, where she could find it upon her return.

Thankfully, Jenny was back at school the next day, fully recovered from what ailed her. I waited with eager and innocent anticipation all day, hoping she would approach me at recess or lunch and let me know she loved me back. But I never heard from her.

Six weeks went by with no word from Jenny. Maybe she couldn't read. Maybe she hated me. Either way, it wasn't good. Then, one day, we were sitting in our small reading group, going over a story about a boy whose grandfather lived in another country. The two were pen pals and wrote to each other monthly. The story was a way to cover the basics of letter writing. As a segue, the teacher stopped to ask if any of us ever had a pen pal or had ever written a letter. No one spoke until Jenny raised her hand.

"I've never written a letter," said Jenny. "But Sam has. Here—look!"

And Jenny pulled out the letter I'd written months earlier and handed it to the teacher. I was momentarily touched that Jenny had kept the letter for this long, and then I was mortified. The teacher was reading the intense feelings I was pouring out in the letter. The teacher was congratulatory, lauding my penmanship and my letter-writing skills, having used proper punctuation for each part. She then proceeded to post the note on the bulletin board so that other students could use it as an example to write their letters for homework.

I had gone for it and it had backfired, of course. But for me and my little second-grade heart, taking a chance by putting it on paper, stuffing it in a school box, and seeing what happened was worth the risk.

What's holding you back? You don't have to climb a mountain, hire a skywriter, or even buy a ring. You just need to let someone know you love them. Don't wait for the perfect moment to come along—create it. You'll find that you don't need a candlelight dinner or romantic music playing in the background. You just need the true feelings and the courage to speak up.

Toss aside your unvoiced love. Let someone know that you love them.

− 32 −
Anything from an infomercial: I know it's late, but you can learn how to chop onions yourself

Infomercials are big business, generating billions of dollars a year in sales during the wee hours of the morning and on weekends. Nearly every product promises to make us happier, healthier, stronger, or sexier, so why not fork over three easy payments of $29.95?

Of course, you don't really need these items. Infomercials trigger impulse buys and make us fill our homes and closets with plastic things that rarely perform as promised. But what can we really do when we're up at 2:00 a.m. and can't sleep? Nothing else is on, there is nothing else to do, and there is no one to talk to. If you can't fall asleep, ordering a presto-matic mop or a sammy-rip-rock paring knife seems like the next best thing.

This is an easy behavior to stop. The next time you find yourself awake at three in the morning, don't turn on the TV. Just don't. Read a book. Research in depth your latest interest. Email a relative or friend you haven't spoken with in a while. Ask yourself some hard questions. Doing any of these things is far more productive than ordering something that cooks an omelet and moonlights as a waffle iron.

Many of us complain about not having enough time or energy to find and pursue our passions. And if insomnia is rare for you, gaining that one hour could pay real dividends in productivity. It could be the hour you find what you've been looking for, learn the one thing that has eluded you, or discover a more relevant way to bring your dreams to reality.

Truth be told, your days are filled with these opportunities already, if you just look for them. Waiting in line, waiting for programs or meetings to start, and waiting in traffic all provide opportunities to learn (and not shop). Education doesn't stop when you graduate; only the formal part of it does. Where and when today can you make some time for learning?

− 33 −
More TVs than people in your house: Don't be afraid of turn-offs

The TV has become a family member in our society. While the per-unit cost has decreased, we still spend a pretty penny on the newest, clearest, sleekest model so we can watch the game, the movie, or the drama we love. It's on during dinner and when we're not even in the room.

Many homes have a TV in every room in the house. Each bedroom has a TV, as does each sitting area, like the family room or the den. And now that online video has become mainstream, as long as a computer is in a room, technically, so is a TV. Why have so many? Do you really need a TV in each room? And when did you cross that line to having more TVs in your home than people? Even if each family member wants to watch something different, there is still a surplus of TV sets. What's the point?

A lot of public awareness campaigns already exist designed to get families and individuals to turn off TV for an entire week. This is a great start, but many people need a more dramatic shift. One solution is to get rid of every TV. As long as it works, you can sell it, earning at least a small amount of cash. More easily, shift your habit and make TV watching a smaller part of your daily routine. It may start with canceling your cable, another way to save a nice amount of money.

We all watch entirely too much TV—TV that is uninspiring, unentertaining, and even degrading. Although difficult and jarring at first, you'll soon forget about what it is you're not watching. Most shows are available for viewing online, so if there is something you feel deeply compelled to watch, you will be able to gain access to it soon and easily enough. Getting out of your monotonous TV routine will free you up to spend time on other, more productive pursuits. And, if you don't think your TV habits are excessive just because you don't have more sets than people, keep a list of how many hours of TV you're watching already. It may alarm you.

It's time that you used TV as a form of recreation and stopped worshipping it. You may miss out on some water cooler conversations with co-workers, but wouldn't you rather talk about your passion than the latest reality show gossip?

TV is something you clearly won't miss—in any form—once you begin to live a life full of passion.

− 34 −
Shiny tennis shoes:
Go away, far away

It seems like more and more people are choosing to walk across America. Many people decide to climb a mountain in order to discover themselves, find a new way of life, or chase down a dream. There are plenty of online videos about people who have traveled around the world or across a country to dance, jog, or hike.

The most beautiful thing about all of these dreamers is that they're willing to get their shoes dirty. In fact, they crave dirty and tarnished shoes, wearing holes in soles because nothing less would have allowed them to wholeheartedly take on such an awesome challenge.

Lots of us want to keep our shoes looking as new as possible when we buy them. This is misguided thinking. Dirty shoes don't tell others that you like to play in the mud. Rather, they serve as evidence that you're ready to hit the road, take on new experiences, and discover something worth exploring. You're eager and willing to get out into this great big world and see what's available to you.

Your feet are just one way to get you where you'd like to be. They provide you with a direct, firsthand experience (as opposed to taking a helicopter tour or watching a TV documentary). Having shoes on the ground means that you can enjoy the smells, meet the people, taste the food, and feel the atmosphere. There's no better way to travel.

The point isn't to walk somewhere. I'd hate for you to spend all the time you save with these 50 suggestions just to take a walk. The point is to get deeply immersed wherever you go, open to learning from your surroundings, as if through osmosis. Your life doesn't need shoes that haven't been soiled, just because you have been unwilling to tromp the muck of everyday life. Coming home from a trip with well-worn shoes is as good a souvenir as you can find. Where will you go and what will you learn?

As long as you're willing to get dirty, the possibilities are endless. The sad reality is that a dedication to cleanliness and protocol prevents so many people from self-discovery. It's okay to have dirty shoes—dirty shoe stories are always more interesting than shiny shoe stories.

− 35 −

Bucket lists: Stop making lists and just do everything you've always wanted to do

I'll start with a disclaimer: I never saw the movie *Bucket List,* so I can't comment on it, nor is this item a critique of the film. That said, your life doesn't need a bucket list. If you want to do something before you die, do it now.

A friend of mine has tried to sell me life insurance for a few years. In an effort to sign me up, he tries to scare me with the hypothetical situation of my getting hit by a bus. What will happen to my family? My finances? Am I prepared? I usually want to tell him how unlikely it is that I will be hit by a bus. I don't go jogging on the freeway or near the bus depot. He would do better with the more likely scenario, "What if you're sitting on your couch, eating a granola bar, and watching Dirty Jobs when . . ." Anything that follows that picture, except perhaps "when a meteor crashes through your roof," has a much higher probability of occurring than my getting hit by a bus.

Most people who make bucket lists use the list to delay doing something now. By saying you want to do something before you die, you can postpone it. Sure—it's good to have goals and it's great to make a list of very ambitious ones that you hope to work toward. But what a shame to make "kicking the bucket" your deadline. You never know when you're going to die, but most of us—unless we're over eighty or have a terminal illness—think and hope that it won't happen for a while yet. Bucket lists have the effect of leaving our deadlines vague. Setting firm dates on any goal means that we must work more actively to reach it.

Ditch the bucket list. Instead, take those lofty goals and unique experiences and set a real deadline. Accomplish five of them this year. Select two more and have them done within the decade. Removing the abstract deadline allows you to focus on the task of bringing them to reality. If you don't meet a deadline, don't sweat it. But don't extend the deadline indefinitely. Figure out what you need (money, time, connections, other people) to accomplish what it is you want to achieve and begin lining up those resources today.

As a result, you will be the most interesting person you know. And think of all that you'll get to do in the next year! You'll go skydiving, run a marathon, crush grapes with your bare feet, write a book, learn to surf, and live in another country! Sounds like a great life, no matter when you go.

— 36 —
Noise:
Find what's informative and get more of it

Our world is full of noise. Silence is unappreciated and even feared. We flip on the TV as soon as we get home just to have something making noise, filling the void of silence. Coffee shops play music and offices pump in white noise. Although music can add ambience and an aesthetic benefit, your life doesn't need more noise.

Noise is any sound that isn't beneficial. People may interpret the word differently (one person's loud music is another person's noise pollution), but the point is to figure out for yourself what is noise and what isn't. For me, noise is anything that doesn't provide information or pleasure.

Most of the talking heads on the 24-hour news

channels are noise. I don't listen to them. Much of what is on the radio is noise, whether it is the sports commentator or elevator music. It will take some time, but finding what podcasts you enjoy, which music you love to bop your head to, and which channels provide the best information will mean that all of your consumption will be beneficial. If it goes in your ears, it will be providing you benefit in the form of entertainment or instruction.

Such a discovery should also motivate you to make sure you're not contributing to the noise in our world. Make sure your words and conversations are constructive and contribute to the good and growth of society. Instruct others, but not in a way that is sanctimonious or bemeaning. Make music you're passionate about that other people will love to hear. Our world has enough arguments and controversy. Do your best not to create more angst; instead, sing beautiful thoughts and speak wise words.

The more you listen to what's not noise, the easier it will be for you to create the same. Like having a good conversation, listen more than you speak. You will soon see that the world around you becomes much more beautiful.

— 37 —
Poor finances:
How not to worry about money ever again

There is a difference between poor finances and being broke. If you're broke, you have no finances, so they can neither be poor nor great. Unfortunately, people sometimes become broke by having poor finances. Your life doesn't need financial mismanagement. Keeping track of your finances will mean that you stay on top of how much money you have, how much money you need, and how much money you want.

I am by no means a financial guru. There are plenty of people who are better suited to giving detailed and sage financial advice. All I know is one basic tenet I've tried to live by since I earned my first paycheck at the age of fifteen: don't spend more than you earn.

Of course, there are times to borrow money, like when you need a house or a car or an education. It's up to you to determine how much you'll need to borrow at any given time. But borrowing for a house or a car or an education in amounts greater than your ability ever to pay back isn't wise. Nor is seeing something you want and immediately buying it. The first question, when you see a shirt or laptop or vacation you want, should not be, "How badly do I want it?" but rather, "Can I afford it?"

If you have money on hand for these nonessential purchases, go for it. If you don't, keep walking. Many of the suggestions in the 50 things can help you avoid temptations to make purchases that can easily stack up on credit cards and take ages to pay off. But if you still find yourself desperately wanting video games, CDs, or books, your only rule of thumb should be whether or not you have the money to pay for them. Now. Not next week when the paycheck comes in or next month when you will have paid off that unexpected car repair. Now.

If the allure of buying things is still too strong, impose a 24-hour waiting period on yourself. Before you buy that purse with all the sequins or that water balloon slingshot, wait 24 hours. If you still want it as badly the next day, do the math and see if it works out. If you don't want it as badly, then don't buy it. If a single day decreases your desire for the thing, it probably wasn't worth buying to begin with.

Use whatever system works for you to keep track of your earnings and what you spend. Use cash in envelopes, a debit card, online software, an abacus—the method doesn't matter. The math does. You know what you earn in a month. As long as you don't spend as much as you earn, you're in good shape. You're in even better shape if you can pin it down even further and plan out what you will need in the month ahead to cover the basics, like rent, food, transportation, and that modem fried by the latest lightning storm. (Especially the modem fried by the latest lightning storm. Life is full of lightning storms.) Whatever is left over is for your enjoyment and to pursue your passion. Don't spend a penny more and you will help ensure that you don't have poor finances—and that you don't go broke.

− 38 −

Someone else's expectations: These are your dreams, not theirs

Tragically, the heaviest expectations we carry on our shoulders are those placed there by other people. We carry them around—sometimes for decades—because we feel compelled to accomplish them or at the very least not abandon the intention of accomplishing them. But the reality is that our lives would be much better if we could simply rid ourselves of them. Your life doesn't need someone else's expectations.

This is your life, after all. Certain people have helped you get where you are, but unless you have some sort of legal documentation, you are free to live your life on your own terms. Find the job you want. Marry the person you love. Move to the city where you want to live. Worship how you choose.

You will let people down. This book is not a guide to making everyone happy. In fact, it's the opposite. This book is a guide to making you happy. It's a way to clear up what isn't needed in your life so that you have time and attention to do what you love and be who you want to be and follow your dreams while living your passion.

So drop them. Let them crash to the floor and shatter. Walk away from the rubble and toward the life you've always wanted. Your dreams should be big enough already. Don't think of it as letting others down. Think of it as making sure you don't crumble under the weight of your dreams and theirs. Life is short and you've only got the time, attention, and resources to accomplish one set of dreams. They may as well be yours—the big, huge, massive dreams that are uniquely yours that you are setting out to bring to reality.

— 39 —
A storage unit:
If you're not using it, lose it

Some people have so much stuff that it won't all
fit in their house. Or their garage. Or their back-
yard. Or under the porch. The decision? They get
a storage unit and cart all of the extra stuff across
town and let it sit in a unit until they need it. Chances are, their life doesn't need nearly everything they
put there. If you have a storage unit, your life probably doesn't need whatever is in it.

It's okay to have a temporary storage unit. You
may be renovating your house and need to move
your couch and other furniture while the construc-
tion crew tears out flooring and installs drywall. But
why put stuff somewhere just to sit around because
you think you may need it? Or are you really so tied
to certain objects that you can't donate them and you

would rather retain ownership? Either way, it is time to make the firm decision that your life doesn't need that thing. Or some things. Or lots of things.

Set a limit. If your house cannot hold it, then you don't need to own it. If you really want to keep it, then find something else to give away. Although you may feel more powerful and important owning lots of things, you will feel better and more organized by eliminating what won't fit inside your four walls. It will also make you take stock of what's worth keeping around. If you are not using it, you may as well lose it.

Our world blurs the lines between utility and idolatry. Gadgets and other conveniences are sold as tools to simplify life when in reality they easily become things we worship, idolize, and long too much for. What is needed, then, is a clear understanding of when something has crossed the line from being a tool that helps you to being a toy that owns you.

Can it really save you time that you can then use to pursue a lifelong passion? Will it make certain tasks easier so that you can save time and energy to spend with loved ones? If so, it may be worth getting (if you have room for it in your house). If not, then you probably don't need it. Setting a limit on the number of toys you buy in a year is a good idea, one that will help you lead a balanced life where you keep what's important in mind at all times.

Sometimes, the only thing standing in the way of living the life you've always wanted is all of your things.

– 40 –
Fast food:
The beauty and agony of getting dinner for $2

The fact that you can get anything to eat at any hour of the day on any corner in America should both excite you and send you into a spiral of questions. Convenience sure is fantastic, as long as you don't wonder what's actually in the value meal you just ordered.

Fast food, as most of us know it, is an excuse to eat and run, scarf down our meal without tasting it, and move on to the next thing on our agenda. Our ancestors would cringe at how most of us eat today, in cars and in front of the TV. No one hunts or gathers dinner, preferring instead that it come in a brown paper sack or a microwaveable tray. Clearly, this is no way to live.

News reports and documentaries have chronicled how unhealthy fast food is. In what seems like a direct response, many restaurants have changed their menus to include fresh fruit, leaner meat, or smaller portions. While ordering an apple from a drive-thru is better than a bag of fries, unless you have a different mindset, you'll continue to deprive yourself of the chance to eat great food.

You may not love cooking, and if preparing food has nothing to do with your passion, I'm not suggesting you go to culinary school. I'm not a dictary expert and I'm not trying to dispense nutritional advice. Rather, I want to highlight the benefits of eating slow meals from local sources and what you might discover if your life doesn't have fast food in it.

Knowing where your food came from is a rarity these days. Strangers behind a counter handing you a burger in a box is hardly a comforting thought. Rather, by going to a farmer's market and meeting those who grow your food, you'll find an appreciation for each potato or egg or strawberry you enjoy afterward. You may even get to hear about someone's passion and someone's career, another rare occurrence in our world.

Skipping fast food means you will be healthier, too. If you only ate cakes or ice cream whenever you actually made them, you would consume far fewer sweets, and eating meals full of grains or protein or vegetables is much healthier than consuming frozen buns that hold chicken injected with hormones and other preservatives. Similarly, by eating food that you prepare in the company of others, you will enjoy not just what you're eating, but with whom you are eating it. Food is rarely a communal experience nowadays, unless you're trying to network over lunch or you are out on a date. Inviting the neighbors over for a cookout, or hosting your co-workers for potluck puts community back into our dinners, just like the community enjoyed by those families Norman Rockwell painted.

Even if you don't care about food, you will find

value in all of these exercises. The discipline that baking teaches or the community that dining together creates are great tools as you seek to live a more passionate life. Sit next to a friend and discuss life over good food and great wine. You'll never want another combo meal again.

— 41 —
Worry:
Spend time correcting problems, not creating more

If I had a magic pill that eliminated worry, I'd stop writing forever and get into the pharmaceutical business. Everyone wants to eliminate worry from his life, whether it consumes almost every thought or it's only a minor distraction when the going gets tough. Very few seem to be able not to worry. Despite the myriad self-help books and resources on the market, part of the human brain seems as if it's wired to worry. Worry is something your life doesn't need, but why? And how can you get rid of it?

Worry is only bad when it paralyzes you from acting. If you are worried about passing a test, the solution isn't to keep worrying; it's to start studying. If you can find the reason for your worry, you will also find the very thing needed to eliminate it: action.

A big test, a job interview, a meeting with the boss, a tough conversation in a relationship—these are all situations that induce worry. Maybe your palms are sweating profusely right now just at the thought of any of those situations. When confronted with the unknown or a decision that needs making, many of us decide the first thing to do is to worry.

I bet that if you ignored this gut response and instead got to work addressing the problem causing the anxiety or worry, you'd eliminate the need to worry in the first place. Star athletes, straight-A students, gifted artists, and strong leaders may feel worry creeping up occasionally. But as soon as they do, they remind themselves that the answer is to confront it using their talents and abilities.

Even though worry seems hard to get out of your life, in reality, it's actually very simple. As worry enters your mind, put yourself to work. Study, practice, research. Get busy. Act. Getting rid of worry never happens by telling yourself to stop. Make yourself so busy that you don't have time to worry. After all, worry is a luxury for people with too much time on their hands.

— 42 —
Seven Deadly Sins:
Put balance in your life

Without going into too much theological detail, the seven deadly sins have been around for more than a thousand years. The list has taken many forms for many reasons, but the commonly agreed upon list points to the sins of wrath, greed, sloth, pride, lust, envy, and gluttony. These seven transgressions are to be avoided at all costs. Different theologies place different punishments upon those who commit these sins, but I don't see these seven sins as a rulebook or a checklist of what not to do. Rather, I see this list as a reminder that life is about balance and going overboard in any area causes us to lose focus from what is important. We humans have a propensity to indulge ourselves in too much of a good thing until it eventually becomes a bad thing. Come to think of it, the writers of these "rule books" probably wrote them, not to rule over us, but to spare us from ourselves.

You can get angry, but you must not let anger consume so much of your life it begins to shape your decisions (wrath).

It's okay to set goals and want to attain fame or wealth. But when the quest for more becomes an end in itself, you've gone overboard and no longer remember why you wanted to be rich or well known in the first place (greed).

It's okay to relax from time to time, but when you blow off responsibilities and indulge only your own desires, you lose focus and are no longer making progress toward your passion (sloth).

When you have accomplished something great, celebrating your achievements is more than acceptable. But when you begin to think of yourself as exceptional or greater than others, a healthy respect of your milestones has gone out the window (pride).

Love is the most beautiful of human emotions and its expressions add happiness to others' lives. But when love becomes nothing more than a sexual pursuit, the object of your affection is lost in the quest for purely physical gratification (lust).

Seeing what someone else has and wanting it for yourself is a very natural feeling. But when that feeling becomes a deep-seated desire and you begin to hate the other person simply for what she owns— and the fact that you don't own it—you've departed from a healthy notion of want (envy).

Enjoying great food or a favorite drink is a wonderful part of being human. But when the love of food or drink supplants the love you have for others and begins to distract you from other responsibilities, you have eaten too much (gluttony).

There is a fine line between utility and idolatry. Something can be a necessary part of your life, but when you begin to worship that thing, instead of use it, something is amiss. The seven deadly sins teach us that. Assign whatever theological or religious significance to them that you wish, but remember that any emotion can become obsessive. Keeping your life in balance is necessary to discovering your passion and beginning to live your life accordingly.

Even too much passion can be a bad thing.

$-43-$
A long commute:
Distance makes the heart
grow angrier

The average American spends over one hundred hours a year getting to work. And more than three million of us spend over three hours getting to and from work each day, far more than a hundred hours a year. Time spent commuting might be worthwhile if we liked our job. Instead, most people hop in cars and on trains to clock in and get started. They complete tasks, schedule meetings, and do all that they can by quitting time just to get back home. Road weary and exhausted, they can't help wondering, "Is it worth it?"

Your life doesn't need a long commute. The only reason you may have one is that living farther from work means you can afford a bigger house.

It seems like a bargain except for the fact that you're losing valuable time you could be spending inside that giant house. Why did you want such a big house anyway? So that you could spend time away from the other people who live there? And we wonder why Americans spend less time with their families and everyone seems to be growing increasingly isolated.

Think about it: 100 hours of drive-time. That's longer than the 40 hours you saved up to take a week's vacation. It's uncompensated time. And if you're off the clock, you shouldn't be stuck in traffic. You ought to be doing something you enjoy, something you're passionate about, or something you've always wanted to try. Worst of all, your daily commute makes you unhappy. You hate it. It's unpredictable, tedious, and even monotonous. And you only hate it more the more you do it. So there it is—a long commute is something you hate, it can get longer at any given moment, and the more days you commute, the more you hate it. There is no silver lining here—not even a free house surrounded by rainbows and trees that grow candy bars.

The only real solution is abstinence. Give up the commute altogether. Technology makes nearly any job doable from your home office—if not daily then at least a few times a week. You could also trade in your house way out yonder for a smaller place closer to your office. This is a bit more complicated than persuading your boss that you can keep up productivity from home, but studies show that those who work from home tend to be more productive than their office-bound counterparts.

Big houses don't make people happier, and long commutes make us angry. (So angry at times that I am reminded of one of the seven deadly sins we examined in Thing 42!) These are two things your life doesn't need. Trade them in and watch your life improve.

– 44 –

Complaints without action: Do something

Sometimes, there is no better stress or tension reliever than letting off some steam by complaining. Yell, stomp your feet, or throw something (as long as it's not at someone's head). Just don't let complaining become a lifestyle, in which you idly vent about what bothers you. Your life doesn't need complaints without action.

If you see a problem, it's okay to be upset. Getting upset and proclaiming your disapproval is a good thing. But complaining should never be the end; it should be the beginning. Complaining should lead to action, whether that means protesting, writing, volunteering, or leading the effort to make it right. Take action when you complain. It's the only way you'll ever stop.

"There oughtta be a law!" you say? Then make one (or call or write or email the people who make them). "That ain't right!" you protest. What is right? What should be done? It's time you get to doing it. There should be a new rule stating that if you complain and don't act, then you're not allowed to complain again. Maybe I'll get to work on that.

People who complain but never act should lose their right to be heard. Whether you simply ignore them when they start moaning and groaning, or whether you challenge them to start doing something to address the object of their dislike, the complainer will soon see the folly of griping about something and not acting.

Things only improve because people act to bring it about. Leaders of movements and revolutions weren't merely complainers. They took action. Many were willing to be ridiculed at best and at worst, executed. The Boston Tea Party was not the work of a few colonials who sat around bemoaning an expensive and bitter cup of tea. It was the work of a movement fomented by the notion that taxation without representation was a grave offense, worthy of action. Had any of them done nothing more than complain, King George could have continued his merry old way.

Thankfully, they decided it was time to get to work, and the world was made better for it. What will you improve? You'll need to move beyond complaining to get it done. The time to act is now.

– 45 –
Lines:
Don't wait around

There is no telling how much time the average person spends waiting in line (I tried looking it up). Whether you're waiting to vote, pay for your groceries, or ride a roller coaster, time spent standing around is time wasted, and your life doesn't need that.

To solve the problem, you could resolve only to go to places and do things that never require a line. This may prove tricky, especially since you can never predict when there will and won't be a line at airport security, at the coffee shop, or at the stadium restroom. Instead, find ways to make your time in line productive. Waiting in line is the perfect time to do any of the following things:

- Catch up on old text messages or voice mails
- Find one person in your phone you haven't spoken with in ages and make a quick call
- Read a magazine or book
- Make a list of what you need to do tomorrow
- Memorize the Bill of Rights
- Listen to a podcast or radio program that makes you smarter
- Reply to emails
- Learn something new
- Meet a stranger (the people in front of and behind you)
- Ask yourself the six questions at the end of this book about discovering your passion

It's impossible to eliminate lines from our society entirely, but we can eliminate the time that is wasted when stuck in them. It may mean you need to bring along a bag in which to carry books, magazines, a music player, or other resources. Such an investment will be worth it as you capitalize on small pockets of time each week that allow you to be more productive than ever before.

One day, when you tell someone the story of how you discovered your passion, it may very well begin with, "I was waiting in line to pump my gas when . . ."

− 46 −
Extra cheese:
Only indulge when it's worth it

Would you like fries with that?" "Would you
like to add extra cheese?" "Would you like to
upgrade to an extra large for just fifty cents more?"
"Would you like to add the extra warranty?"

These questions have become needless suggestions in our world. Business ploys to help the bottom
line, adding an extra this or an upgraded that means
you're spending more money for something you
don't really want and don't even need. Start declin-
ing the extras—your life doesn't need them.

Not only will saying "no" help you to save
money a few dollars at a time, it will also help you
remember what is important. Unless you're crazy
about cheese or french fries, you derive no extra
pleasure or benefit from the additional quarter you

forked over. This, of course, begs a larger, more introspective question: Do you know what you like? Do you know what you love?

Your life doesn't have room for you to be in love with hundreds of ideas, things, or foods. Find the handful of pursuits you're willing to sacrifice for and apply your hard-earned dollars and time to them. Skipping the cheese on your burger will save you some cash, but it will also serve as a reminder of what is really important. If you are trying to start a company, finish a degree, complete a marathon, or build a family, these pursuits can't be done haphazardly or as an afterthought. Anything less than total dedication jeopardizes your ability to succeed.

Getting rid of extra cheese isn't just about making sure your life isn't nickeled and dimed. It's about making sure you know your most important commitments and never waver. Being committed to a cause, a goal, a profession, or a person is a noble pursuit and making sure insignificant details don't get in your way is one way to keep these dreams topmost in mind.

Saying no to the cheese is important—it reinforces the significance of what we've said yes to.

— 47 —
A job you hate:
Turn your passion into your profession

Fewer than half of all Americans actually like their jobs. Year after year, fewer people love the work they do. This is mostly a commentary on how we all view the word work and how our world structures it. Of course, it's called "work" for a reason— no one would do it for free, so your company had to pay someone to get the job done. In other words, it isn't easy and it isn't glamorous.

Just because something is difficult or dirty doesn't mean that one cannot take pride or find enjoyment in it. Reality shows about work have shown that some of the happiest people on the planet are those who go home covered in muck at the end of the day. Their secret isn't necessarily in working outside or having flexible hours. Rather, people who are happy in their careers have simply found one that works for them. Life is too short and it doesn't need a job you hate.

Workplace culture is changing; there is no doubt about it. A new generation of workers, technological tools, and a knowledge-based economy of free agent experts have companies changing work habits and patterns. But finding a job you love isn't just about cafeterias serving organic food or loving the people you share an office with. It's about finding a job you can be excited about, something that might even indulge a core passion of yours each and every day you go to work.

The people I know who truly love their jobs do so because they have found something rewarding, challenging, or unique that they're happy to do for several hours a day. Instead of simply looking for a paycheck, look for one of these characteristics in your next employment opportunity:

Rewarding—What about your job is rewarding? Is it the paycheck or the perks? Are you someone who measures rewards in money (it's okay if you do)? If so, what amount for what kind of work makes something rewarding for you? It's important to know this before you apply for your next gig.

Or, do you measure rewards in some other way? Do you derive a sense of purpose from your work that motivates you to complete your tasks each day? Maybe you have a job where you get to make people happy or you provide some kind of social service that helps people meet their basic needs. These goals could make your job rewarding, and make you happy doing it.

Challenging—Does your job stretch you? Are you learning something new, exploring something, or being mentally invigorated? Being stimulated emotionally or mentally will help you to love your job. Going to work knowing that you'll learn something new or leave satisfied at the end of the day could help you love your work a bit more.

Maybe you face some other challenge at work. Clearly, not all obstacles are challenging in a beneficial way. Having a boss who doesn't care about you or working in an industry that you consider morally bankrupt may present challenges, but not the ones that provide enough stimulation to make working worthwhile. These aren't challenges to be overcome and to learn from; they are depressing realities that are difficult to alter. Make sure you find the right challenges at work and wake up each morning knowing that you will be happy with a new problem or task that will be thrown at you later that day.

Unique—Many people love their work because it is unique in some way. Maybe it's uniquely suited to their skill set or a rare job that needs doing. Standing out from the crowd can make work a very happy place to be.

Unique jobs can also exist when you create them. Although not everyone needs to turn her passion into a profession, it will make perfect sense for some. Is it time for you to create the job you've always wanted? Will being your own boss provide you the appropriate amount of financial and emotional stability? Are you disciplined and motivated enough to build your own workplace? And if you do, will you enjoy it along the way?

Work is a major part of your adult life, and hating it is no way to spend all of your years until retirement. Leave a job you don't like and find one you love. It's out there.

– 48 –
Perfection:
Why good enough can be pretty awesome

No one is perfect. Of course, we expect plenty of people to be perfect, and we're genuinely shocked and disappointed when we find them to be anything but. Perfection is an ideal, not a reality. It's a standard to be set and a goal to be striven for, but falling short of that benchmark is not a cause for disappointment. If you strive only for perfection and are upset when you don't achieve it,,you will spend time and energy on a futile pursuit, resources that could be put to better use by making something good enough.

Baseball has "perfect" games, where the pitcher allows no batter to reach base. Students make perfect scores on SATs. Other than these examples and a handful of others, perfection isn't even possible. What does a perfect football game look like? What about a perfect quarter in business or a perfect election result? Many industries and parts of life have no standard of perfection. It's okay if you don't either. This is not an excuse, however, to lower your standards to the point that mediocrity is acceptable or the commonplace is justified. Rather, it's an admonition to set a standard of excellence that you strive to maintain.

Companies and athletes and politicians and artists know when something is excellent, exemplary, or extraordinary. Strive for those adjectives. Try to be interesting, compelling, fantastic, or wonderful. Be remarkable. Don't try to be perfect. It'll never happen and you will spend a lot of time uselessly trying to get there after you've already achieved excellence.

It's okay to lower some standards so long as you are still achieving greatness. Very few people even make it that far, so celebrate when you do.

What does excellence look like for you at work or at home? Define it on paper so you know when you have attained it. When you do, celebrate it and continue to establish a consistent work ethic that pursues excellence instead of perfection.

If you don't strive for excellence, you may not even reach mediocrity.

– 49 –
Unvisited or former friends: Put the "Face" in Facebook

People drift apart. It's the inconvenient truth of many relationships. Former co-workers, people you attended summer camp with, childhood friends, and old classmates all move on to other things. People grow up, get married, move to distant cities, start families, and create entirely new social networks. Before you know it, the people you know become the people you once knew.

Facebook and other social networks curb the impact of drifting, but do not eradicate it. Just because you can see pictures of a friend's new baby doesn't really bring you any closer as individuals. You may be able to see the highlights of someone's life, but you no longer experience the ordinary occurrences that made the two of you friends.

The solution isn't to try to be best buddies with everyone you have ever considered a friend. Rather, you should try to keep alive those friendships that mean the most to you. Your life doesn't need more strangers. Friendship is special, and like most great things in life, you may take it for granted, not appreciating all it offers until it disappears. What friendships do you currently consider most dear or most rewarding? How much time and attention are you giving them?

The same is true with family relationships. Whom should you visit, to minimize the effects of time and distance? Who deserves a special call or letter? Friendships are work, certainly, but the rewards and benefits are well worth the time and energy invested. The best way to make sure an important relationship doesn't end is to make sure it never gets interrupted.

~ 50 ~
This book:
My publisher may hate me, but I've got to be honest

Once you read the next part of this book—about how to find your passion now that you have found more time to focus on it—you have my permission to get rid of the book. Don't return it (the publisher and I have provided you a service worth paying for, I hope), but you can try to sell it on eBay or at a used bookstore. I really hope that you pass it on to a friend who is searching for his passion. Of course, you're welcome to keep *50 Things,* especially if you have underlined and highlighted a lot of handy reminders or ideas you found. But getting rid of this book is totally okay with me. Now that you have read it, your life doesn't need it.

For starters, you may have too many books on

your shelf. Adding one more may not seem like much, but I hope your shelves are full of books you haven't read instead of books you have. A fully read library has no potential—you already know what is in it. Stacks of unread books, however, carry the potential to improve your world. So now that you have read the book, unless there is something in it you need to keep handy, let someone else enjoy the potential of finding her passion. Use the empty slot on your shelf for another book you plan to read that could broaden your horizons.

I also hope this book has served its purpose. I hope this list of 50 things your life doesn't need has allowed you to find more time, money, and energy to pursue your passions with reckless abandon. And I hope that you use the next part of this book to articulate your passion and live your life in pursuit of it. Once you find your passion, you will realize that everything else can go. Figuring out what is important—those one, two, or a handful of things that really matter more than anything else—means that everything else pales in comparison and your life literally doesn't need it. If you have been able to do that, then a well-worn copy of this book is useless. Time is wasting. Give this book to a friend and get started living your passion.

You have one life. Do something.

Conclusion:
Now that life is simpler, it's time to find your passion

How to find your passion? Now that you have purged your life of everything it doesn't need, you should have more time, money, energy, and resources to find your passion. And even though you may never turn it into your job, you can still begin to live your life full of passion and purpose.

A passion is something that can be clearly articulated. You cannot simply be passionate about music—you must be passionate about doing something with music. Passion is active; it is always in motion. Finding it is a journey, and the next six questions will help you along this path.

Perhaps getting rid of the 50 things your life doesn't need stirred something within you. Maybe a few things on the list piqued an interest that had been dormant within you, or maybe some items brought a new idea to light and you're now very curious about learning or doing more.

These next six questions can be asked time and again as you discover and rediscover your passion. They are questions not to be taken lightly, but to be lived deeply. Ask them of yourself and answer honestly and completely. If you cannot articulate an answer immediately, don't worry. Some of these questions you may be able to answer with a snap and others may take a bit longer. Rest assured knowing that when you are able to answer each one, you will have found your passion, your life's calling, and the very thing that motivates you more than anything else.

Six questions to ask yourself

Question 1: *What do I spend time thinking about the most?*

Granted, if you are a teenage boy, the answer may be sex, sports, or sex. And if you are a teenage girl, the answer may also be sex, sports, or sex. Heck—if you're of any age you could answer this question with those three things. The objective here is to remove from your mind selfish and recreational interests—especially if they do not connect you to something deeper, lasting, and more memorable.

For example, you may think about fishing more than anything else. You go fishing each weekend and holiday, you watch fishing shows on TV, and all of your online friends know you as "that guy who always posts status updates about fishing." Although this may seem like a recreational pursuit, it could also be a passion. Don't dismiss it just because it seems trivial or extracurricular. It could be the very thing you are called to do.

It is important to try to answer this question over a period of time. Jot down each evening what you thought about the most over the course of the day. Do it each day for a week. Then, you can review it after seven days and see if there were any repeated thoughts or themes. For better balance, do it for a month or over a period of time when you're doing different things, like working, vacationing, trying something new, or developing a routine.

Likewise, the same set of things may truly occupy your thoughts, but may not quite be your passion. If you're a parent, a spouse, a supervisor, a teacher, or an artist, most of your days are occupied with similar thoughts. They have to be if you plan to excel in one or more of those roles. Therefore, quantity of time doesn't necessarily indicate a passion.

Instead, in your free time, take note of where your mind goes. If you have some down time in the evening once the kids are tucked in, what is it that comes to mind? If your commute to work is your best chance at time alone, are you pondering something in particular? Lying in bed at night, what do you think about? Or when you are not thinking about anything else, what is it you think about?

If you are willing to be fully in tune with your

thoughts, you will notice that a pattern begins to emerge, something you cannot ignore, something that will start speaking to you.

Question 2: *If I'm known for only one thing, what is it?*

Each of us has only one life—what will it be known for? What will we pack into it? And what will others say about us and the one life we lived? You can answer this question in two ways:

1. What you would currently be known for, were you to die before tomorrow morning.
2. What you'd like to be known for, assuming you get to live a long and normal life, to the ripe old age of 75 or 80.

The second answer should hold the attention of most people, since odds are that you will survive into tomorrow, and because if you knew you wouldn't, you would be very busy settling your affairs in order to get everything done by daybreak.

Your answers to this question may be a bit vague and may also hit on things not related to your passion. That's okay. This question is designed to get you to think in terms bigger than what you do for a living. Unless you are a captain of industry or a world-famous inventor, what you will be known for doing as a career will probably go unknown in most circles, or at least in the circles that are most important to you.

Most of us want to be known as a loving husband, a great wife, a fantastic grandparent, a meaningful friend, or a great son or daughter. We may also want to be thought of as a reliable volunteer, a generous giver, or a visionary board member. Deep down, what is it you want to be known for?

This question will also be best answered if you think about how you'd like to be known by different people. By thinking intentionally about these audiences, you'll also be honest about who means more to you. It is more important that your parents think of you as a fantastic son than your customers think of you as a smart marketer. And it's more important that your friends consider you as someone who is supportive than strangers who read your Wikipedia entry consider you to be a strategic innovator.

By answering this question, you should think not only of what you'd like to be known for, but also by whom you'd like to be known for it. When you answer this question honestly, you will also discover how important your passion is both to you and those around you.

Question 3: *What do I value?*

Almost everyone has a moral compass. Most of society has an idea of right and wrong. But very few of us have a clearly defined set of values, those things that guide us to make decisions about what is right and wrong or what determines true north on our moral compass.

Perhaps it is a lack of knowing what you value that leads you down slippery slopes and morally ambiguous paths. Understanding what it is you treasure most and then making decisions in light of those priorities will enable you to stay on course when it comes to defining and then acting on your calling. While value systems and even ethics can differ from one person to the next, making sure that you have an understanding of your own system will help you discover what's important, what's worth spending time on, and where you are willing to make a stand—the three components of a clearly defined answer to this question.

What one person considers essential or urgent could be what another thinks is worthless or even comical. If you're not sure what is important to you, however, you will never know what you value and you may never arrive at knowing what it is you were born to do. Think about what you value. What is it that you consider urgent, necessary, or deserving of your full attention? Is there a certain issue, news story, or idea that always captivates you and makes you stop what you are doing in order to fully engage? Is there something that will always motivate, inspire, or challenge you? If you were to list five things that you consider important, what would they be and why?

Another way to think about what you value is to take stock of what you spend time on. What in your life do you make sure to do right or do well regardless of the time it takes? What will you make sure to stay up late or wake up early for in order to complete or accomplish? Answering this question—perhaps more than the other two—will also bring to light what it is you don't value. Then, you can begin to let those things go or fall to the wayside in order to better devote time and energy toward what it is you value and might just be called to do. If you don't value or appreciate something and if you don't consider something important, then why spend time on it, time you could devote to honing an existing talent, growing an essential resource, or further following your passion?

Along with considering something important and then spending time on it, you must think about where you're willing to take a stand. While you could answer this question in political or religious terms, you could also answer it in terms of a social issue, a particular hobby, or an educational pursuit. In other words, what do you correct others about when someone is misinformed? When are you willing to attach your name and identity to an opinion you have? When are you willing to stand alone, stick your neck out, or go out on a limb? What is it that motivates you to make a commitment and then invite others to make that same commitment?

Question 4: *What must I do every day?*

Although this question can seem a lot like Question 3, especially in terms of where you take a stand or how you spend your time, it's important to remember that consistent and repeated action is often a key indicator of where we're passionate.

Taking a stand in the form of having and sharing an opinion (especially online) is one thing. Carving out time to focus on or think about it is another.

Making sure to engage in an active, regular, and—best of all—daily discipline could help you more easily zero in on a passion.

Some things you do every day, like showering, eating, and breathing. You're probably also going to work, paying bills, and being a responsible member of society. But for this question, think beyond what it is you have to do and more along the lines of what you want to do. What is it that you enjoy doing more than anything else? Is there something you do when you leave work that you think about? What is your favorite part of the day? What is it, after you do it, that you tell everyone about? Is there something that's a regular part of your day that you can't do without? Is there a certain routine that if interrupted throws you out of whack for the rest of the day?

There are activities that you do every day that you love, so be sure to think critically about this question. We all love spending time with friends and loved ones, and hopefully you get to do this each day, whether it is in person or virtually. But it would be very hard to make a living at visiting with friends or to even assume that this is what you were born to do. Think carefully and thoughtfully. What do you freely choose to do each day that is not required but that you feel must be a part of your day for it to be complete? It's okay to admit that you feel that you must do this thing, almost as though it were an obligation, when trying to define your passion.

Question 5: *What do I tell other people about myself?*

Cocktail parties and mixers can be the worst place in the world to go if you're still trying to figure out your passion. Anywhere you go and are forced to meet people, you will be asked, "What do you do?" This is often, of course, a bad question. No one wants to be defined in anyone's mind by what he does to earn a paycheck, unless, of course, what he does is his passion. If you are forced to answer, "I work at a job I hate," or "I sit on the phone all day," or "I do something that you think is stupid, meaningless, or insignificant," then you immediately hate the person asking, the event you're attending, or yourself. You could decide never to go to parties or anywhere else that you may meet someone you don't know, or you could change the question or the answer—or both.

When I meet new people, I like to ask either, "What's your story?" or "What would you like me to know about you?" This way, if people want to tell me how they are able to pay for groceries, so be it. But it also opens the door for connection on a deeper, more passionate level. It means that we can get past nametags and get down to what it is each of us cares about and spends time doing. Immediately, a sense of passion can come to the forefront.

You can answer this question by answering either of the ones that I ask at parties. What is your story? And what would you like a total stranger to know about you? Is it what you're passionate about or what you're called to do? Is it where you'd like to be or what you'd like to be remembered for? You will also find that by answering this question—whether at parties or on a sheet of paper—you will have more meaningful conversations and connections, which is always time well spent.

How do you introduce yourself in new situations? How would you like to be known by others?

Question 6: *When do I feel fulfilled?*

The reason I shy away from terms like happiness or excitement when talking about passion is that those terms can be very temporary. Even if your passions change over the course of your lifetime, they take root in something much more permanent.

And that's why this final question asks about fulfillment, instead of just asking about happy and exciting times. Fulfillment is a condition that can last much longer than happiness. It's a feeling that brings with it a sense of accomplishment and completeness. It's something that can make you proud and leave you feeling like you did something that was worth doing. Fulfillment carries a sense of purpose, not just a feeling of elation or entertainment. Your passion, therefore, isn't based on simple mood; it transcends your mood on any given day and shapes your outlook and mindset, keeping you fulfilled and with a sense of purpose no matter how you may be feeling.

This is also a helpful reminder that a passion is very different from an interest. Interests come and go, often changing with age or life circumstance. Some interests will blossom into full-blown passions, but not all of them. Likewise, you shouldn't spend too much time on a mere interest—it can take away from the time you could be spending living out your passion. Indulge an interest that makes you happy, but be willing to sacrifice it in an instant for a passion that brings you deep fulfillment.

Which behaviors or actions bring a sense of fulfillment for you? What do you do that, when you do it, makes you feel proud for having completed the task? What will you tell others later that you did today? Knowing what brings fulfillment will help you prioritize how you spend your time. This is important, because determining your passion and how exactly you would like to devote your life to it will require all the time you can give it.

Now that you have found your passion, you have the great responsibility of living it. This is the next wonderful journey ahead of you. Whether or not your passion ever changes, what you have just defined is now part of you, and being true to yourself demands that you live life to the fullest.

Take the next step and live your passion boldly. Your life doesn't need anything less.

About Cool People Care

Founded in 2006 by Sam Davidson and Stephen Moseley, Cool People Care has a simple mission: to save the world. Through the Internet and by email, Cool People Care has already connected thousands of nonprofit organizations with local supporters. CoolPeopleCare.org has been visited by people in more than 150 countries and currently holds more than 2,000 ways to make a difference in the world in your daily life. The company also offers a complete line of eco-friendly and fundraising merchandise, for sale on its Web site, which has raised more than $100,000 for various charities around the United States. To learn more, visit CoolPeopleCare.org.

Check out these other books in the things *series:*
good
to know™

5 Things to Know for Successful and Lasting Weight Loss
(ISBN: 9781596525580, $9.99)

12 Things to Do to Quit Smoking
(ISBN: 9781596525849, $9.99)

20 Things To Know About Divorce
(ISBN: 9781596525993, $9.99)

21 Things To Create a Better Life
(ISBN: 9781596525269, $9.99)

24 Things to Increase the Emotional Intelligence of Your Man
(ISBN: 9781596527393, $9.99)

27 Things To Feng Shui Your Home
(ISBN: 9781596525672, $9.99)

27 Things To Know About Yoga
(ISBN: 9781596525900, $9.99)

29 Things To Know About Catholicism
(ISBN: 9781596525887, $9.99)

30 Things Future Dads Should Know About Pregnancy
(ISBN: 9781596525924, $9.99)

30 Things Future Moms Should Know About How New Dads Feel
(ISBN: 9781596527607, $9.99)

33 Things To Know About Raising Creative Kids
(ISBN: 9781596525627, $9.99)

34 Things To Know About Wine
(ISBN: 9781596525894, $9.99)

35 Things to Know to Raise Active Kids
(ISBN: 9781596525870, $9.99)

35 Things Your Teen Won't Tell You, So I Will
(ISBN: 9781596525542, $9.99)